DIRTY POLITICS

A–Z of trickery, treachery and other tasty treats

DIRTY POLITICS

A–Z of trickery, treachery and other tasty treats

Pan Macmillan acknowledges the Traditional Custodians of Country throughout Australia and their connections to lands, waters and communities. We pay our respect to Elders past and present and extend that respect to all Aboriginal and Torres Strait Islander peoples today. We honour more than sixty thousand years of storytelling, art and culture.

First published 2025 by Macquarie Dictionary Publishers,
an imprint of Pan Macmillan Australia Pty Ltd
1 Market Street, Sydney, New South Wales, Australia 2000

ISBN: 9781761773952

Cover image: Bill Hope / The Jacky Winter Group
Cover design: Natalie Bowra
Typeset by Natalie Bowra
Printed by IVE

Many thanks to Melissa Kemble for citations and verification of sources, and to Gus Wheeler and Rebecca Geddes from Macquarie Dictionary for their editorial assistance.

A Cataloguing-in-Publication entry is available from
the National Library of Australia
http://catalogue.nla.gov.au

Contents

Where were you when you first heard the word 'gerrymander'?

I'll go first: I was sitting in my Year 10 politics class, watching my indefatigable teacher Mr Gurry bravely battling to hold our attention. No mean feat, considering this was 1999 and the internet had just arrived at school.

But something about this word and its backstory piqued my interest: how in 1812 the Governor of Massachusetts, Elbridge Gerry, oversaw a redistribution of the political map to give his own party a considerable advantage. The resulting district resembled a salamander (according to newspaper cartoonists) and editors wasted no time in creating the perfect portmanteau. Because why call it 'carving up an electoral map for political gain' when you can simply call it a 'gerrymander?'

Perhaps it was just the heady fumes of Lynx Africa, but my fifteen-year-old brain was thrilled to discover this word. Not only was it fun to say, but it was laden with history, irony and truth-telling: a shorthand way of calling bullshit on our elected leaders and the lengths they'll go to in order to retain power.

Civics education is waning in Australia, but I dare say if the department of education boffins were brave enough to insert the words 'jeffed', 'woketard' and 'ratfuck' into the national curriculum we'd suddenly have a whole generation of young people freshly engaged in the history of privatisation, culture wars and bilateral relations.

And if you're new to these words, don't worry – you're holding the perfect book. It is my hope that readers of all ages will have their very own 'gerrymander' moment as they learn of our finest linguistic leaps, and discover that our leaders are generally more poorly behaved than a classroom of rowdy fifteen-year-olds.

– Sammy J
Satirical comedian, writer and composer

The disconnect between what Australians want from their politicians (and have every right to expect) and how they actually regard them has never been greater. Polling data regularly shows that politicians at every level of government are among the least trusted in the country – keeping company at the bottom with everyone's favourite: real estate agents.

This comes as no surprise. We all know that actions speak louder than words, and the broken promises, scandals and controversies have done nothing to assuage Australia's natural cynicism towards authority figures. But our trust issues aren't founded only in the divide between actions and words. Our confidence in the very meanings of those words has been shaken.

We now have a relentless 24-hour news cycle and countless social media platforms to publicise and replay every misstep a public figure makes – in both their public and private lives. Sound bites and political pointscoring are now what holds value, seemingly to the detriment of constructive policy-making, bipartisanship and properly addressing long-term key issues.

It is Macquarie Dictionary's role to record language as it is used within Australian English – from the colourfully colloquial to the highly technical – across different registers and subject areas – and not just the urban centres but to the far reaches of regional Australia. While this may come as a surprise to many whose only political education was their Year 6 school excursion to Parliament House, the amount and range of language used both within and of the political arena is rich and diverse.

This book has resulted from a deep-dive into Macquarie's Word of the Year archives. In turn, we've been both shocked and entertained by what has been revealed in assembling past political contenders and winners. The Word of the Year started back in 2006. While the playful Australian creation 'muffin top' took out the overall winning spot in that inaugural year, the winner of the politics category was worryingly 'plausible deniability' – a term which we've seen steadily increase in usage over the past 20 years. It is a rare year when the editors are scrabbling to find interesting contenders for our politics category.

The A–Z content presents a tongue-in-cheek look at the language many of us have unknowingly had at our fingertips to describe the underbelly of politics. Yet it is the wild barbs and outlandish quotes from the politicians themselves that never fail to sting and entertain. Who really is the king of the bedwetters? Who got slapped by warm cabbage? And who made up the conga line of suckholes?

While our political landscape has left many of us jaded and disillusioned, we hope this book will make you laugh. In bringing all of the 'darker' and more 'unseemly' of these behaviours and practices to light, Macquarie is presenting us all with a chance to rap the knuckles of and tut-tut our governing representatives simply by presenting the lexicon for scrutiny.

– *Victoria Morgan*
Executive Editor | Macquarie Dictionary

We are not interested in the views of painted, perfumed gigolos. We are not interested in the Gucci image and the rest. We are interested in making Australia work.

Paul Keating on John Hewson
House of Representatives, Hansard, 6 June 1984

adhocracy

a government which acts with unthinking immediacy in its responses to events, influences, etc.

Such kneejerk or ad hoc reactions typically result in a **bandaid solution**.

adventurism

recklessness, rash improvisation or experimentation, especially in politics or finance.

alternative fact

a false statement presented as fact, especially one made in a political context.

The term was popularised in 2017 by Kellyanne Conway, US political adviser to then president Donald Trump – in regards to the following statement.

> *This was the largest audience to ever witness an inauguration, period, both in person and around the globe.*
>
> – White House Press Secretary Sean Spicer on Donald Trump's 2017 inauguration

-archy

a word element from Greek meaning 'rule' or 'government'.

While familiar in terms such as **monarchy**, **oligarchy** and **anarchy**, the suffix has most recently been used to reflect the rise of the **broligarchy** – government by a group of wealthy men, especially those who occupy prominent roles in the technology sector.

astroturfing

a deliberately organised marketing campaign for a politician, policy or party, falsely presented as having emerged naturally from word of mouth.

attack dog

an aggressive, pugnacious person, especially a parliamentarian whose role is to attack the opposition.

The term can be used interchangeably with the breeds of large dogs, such as the **Doberman**, **Rottweiler**, or **pit bull**, in particular, those breeds that are regarded as aggressive.

> I am not like the Leader of the Opposition. I did not slither out of the Cabinet room like a mangy maggot and then go and leak to the Press a story about how I was beaten by Malcolm Fraser...
>
> – Paul Keating on John Howard, House of Representatives, 17 October 1985

The contrast to the **attack dog** is the poor **poodle** – preferably a **mincing poodle** – who is seen as weak and ineffective.

Aussie battler

a typical member of the Australian working class who has to struggle hard to make a living. Also known as the **little Aussie battler**.

Politicians constantly try to align themselves with the **Aussie battler**. This is where a good **log cabin story** can come in handy.

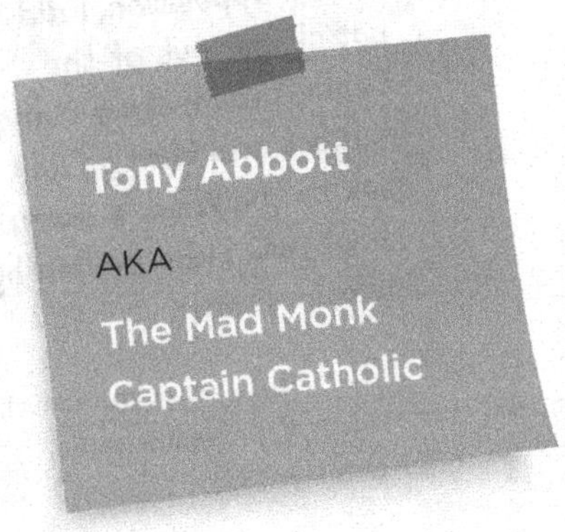

I mean, you know, people are entitled to their sexual proclivities. Let there be a thousand blossoms bloom, as far as I'm concerned. But I ain't spending any time on it because at the moment, every three months, a person is torn to pieces by a crocodile in North Queensland.

Bob Katter
ABC News, 29 November 2017

baby kissing

the kissing of babies in the crowd as part of a public relations exercise, especially in political campaigning.

A practice highly recommended by any good **spin doctor**.

backbite

to denigrate or malign someone in their absence.

backflip

to make a complete reversal in opinion or policy, especially in official policy.

While very similar, the **backflip** is performed much quicker and more decisively than the **backtrack**. **Backflipping** is especially popular just prior to, or following, an election.

background

often used in the phrase **to background against**, to secretly research the actions or activities of a political opponent with the intention of leaking any damaging information to the media.

Any damaging information being collated into a **dirt file** or **dirt dossier**.

You boxhead you wouldn't know. You are flat out counting past 10.

— Paul Keating on Wilson Tuckey, House of Representatives, 21 August 1985

backstab

to do harm to someone, especially someone defenceless or unsuspecting, as by making a treacherous attack on their reputation.

While some politicians prefer the traditional **backstabber** role, a brave few have openly embraced the method of **front-stabbing**. At least there's some transparency for the voters there. Either way it's done, it featured prominently between 2010 and 2018 with the revolving door of six prime ministers.

backtrack

to withdraw from an undertaking or position.

Also, regularly called a **walk back** but considered to be more tentative than a **backflip**.

Balmain basketweavers

a derogatory phrase used to describe left-wing trendies. See **trendy**.

Popularised by Paul Keating in his description of the sort of people who watch the SBS. The inner-city Sydney suburb of Balmain being well known for such inhabitants. Also referred to as **basketweavers from Balmain**.

backchannel

an unofficial means of communication which circumvents official channels, especially as used for the purpose of informal or secret discussions or negotiations.

Here **transparency** is considered a dirty word.

> *The Herald commends Home Affairs Minister Clare O'Neil for suspending Pezzullo less than a day after The Sydney Morning Herald, The Age and 60 Minutes revealed that he spent years using a political backchannel to two Liberal prime ministers to undermine political and public service enemies, promote the careers of conservative politicians he considered allies and lobby to muzzle the press. The prime minister's promise to 'expedite' an inquiry into the revelations from this masthead is also welcome.*
>
> – *The Sydney Morning Herald*, 26 September 2023

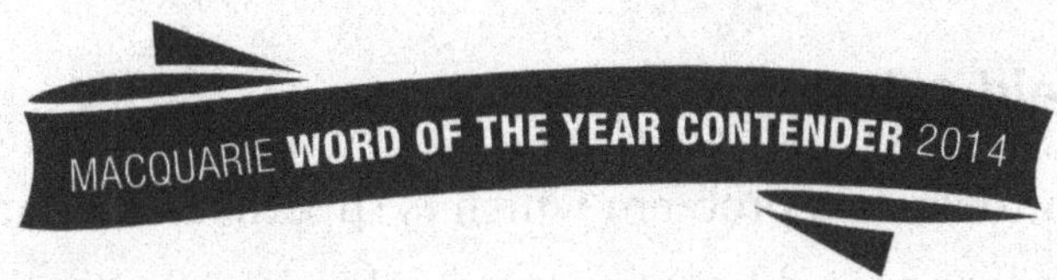

bamboo ceiling

a barrier created by prejudice which hampers the progress of Asian Australians to positions of leadership in government and business institutions.

Modelled on the phrase **glass ceiling**.

> *Ms Long says Australia is starting to pay attention to cultural diversity, but is still far behind the United States. "Australia has a pipeline [of culturally diverse talent] — but they hit the bamboo ceiling and we do not see them [being appointed] as leaders of organisations."*
>
> – ABC News, 2 December 2021

banana republic

any country considered as backward, especially one which is politically unstable and dependent on the trade of rich foreign nations.

Not to be confused with Australia's own **Banana Republic** – the state the **banana benders** come from – Queensland.

bandaid solution

an answer to a problem which is superficial by nature and does not address fundamental issues. See **social bandaid**.

bandwagon effect

the tendency for a party or a particular point of view to gain support because it appears to be on the winning side.

Particularly noticeable during election periods.

barbecue stopper

a topic of conversation or issue for discussion which is of general concern, especially one of political significance.

Coined by our very own John Howard back in 2002. The topics are often strategically deployed in political discourse in attempts to influence public opinion. Australia's more politically focused form of a **water-cooler topic**.

barnstorm

to conduct a vigorous political campaign in rural regions, making many stops and frequent speeches.

If the candidate is from the National Party of Australia then this would be along the **wombat trail**.

bean counter

an accountant or person similarly responsible for budgets.

... the only type of man who can be happy in the job of Treasurer is one who by nature is a sadist and has a heart of stone.

– Harold Holt, The Sydney Morning Herald, 25 July 1959

bearpit

an arena for fierce political debate, as a parliament or a council chamber.

bedwetter

a person who is excessively nervous, timid, fearful, etc. Also, **pants-wetter**.

While this is something you'd only expect to hear in the schoolyard, **bedwetter** is often used to liken politicians to children who wet the bed out of fear or anxiety. To be especially mature about this you could call someone '*captain of the bedwetters*', as former radio broadcaster Alan Jones did to James McGrath, with James replying '*I think you are the king of the bedwetter{s} actually*'.

big government

government that is large in terms of spending capacity and employment, and which has a wideranging impact on the lives of the governed, as by regulatory activities, etc.

Big government is typically seen as being excessively and unnecessarily involved with citizens' lives.

bitch and fold

a strategy in which a member of an opposition party vehemently and publicly criticises a policy proposed by the government, only to ultimately vote in favour of the policy in order for it to pass.

Criticism for criticism's sake until history needs a

rewrite with claims of how congenial and bipartisan they've been.

bleeding-heart liberal

a person of left-wing or liberal views who is deemed to be excessively sensitive and holding a distorted, soft-hearted point of view.

Often perceived by some as **woke**.

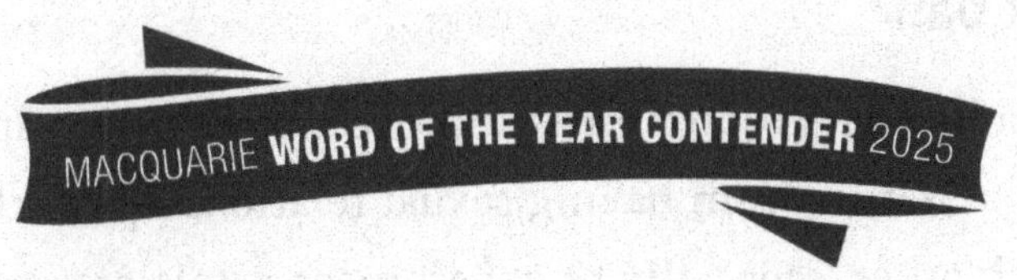

bird-dogging

the act of confronting a politician at a public event with direct questions or issues, with the aim of bringing attention to a specific issue or to call them to account.

This term relates back to the behaviours of a 'bird dog', also known as a 'gundog' – a dog trained to help hunters in locating, flushing and retrieving game birds and other game animals.

Climate activists plan to disrupt politicians' election campaign appearances by reviving "bird dogging", a tactic used to interfere with media appearances from Treasurer Jim Chalmers, Opposition Leader Peter Dutton and shadow treasurer Angus Taylor this week alone.

– *Sydney Morning Herald*, 22 March 2025

bonk ban

a policy which prohibits employees within the same organisation from having sexual relationships with each other, especially of government ministers and their staff.

The term was popularised in 2018 when the policy was introduced as part of the ministerial code of conduct by prime minister, Malcolm Turnbull. We have the deputy prime minister, Barnaby Joyce, to thank for bringing interdepartmental bonking to an end (at least officially) after the very public revelations of his extramarital, extracurricular affair.

Beyond forcing everyone to get and stay married, Malcolm Turnbull's idea of a bonk ban between politicians and staffers had merit. I was not the

> *only one to think it was useful. As former Howard staffer and knife-sharp political commentator Paula Matthewson wrote at the time: 'The sensible sanction will improve workplace conditions and help to lift the standard of behaviour in ministerial offices.'*
>
> – *Canberra Times*, 16 October 2020

Our US counterparts have faced similar problems but instead of putting things bluntly, they shy away from using the term **bonk**.

> *I did not have sexual relations with that woman, Miss Lewinsky.*
>
> – Bill Clinton on Monica Lewinsky, 26 January 1998

> *I didn't have sex with a porn star, number one.*
>
> – Donald Trump on Stormy Daniels, 27 June 2024

boodle

a bribe or other illicit gain in politics.

The **boodler** can also obtain money dishonestly by **boodling**.

boondoggle

an extravagant project which consumes government funds but is of no real value to the public.

The two examples regularly referenced by this term are **Snowy 2.0** and **submarine contracts.**

boys' club

a male clique, especially in business and politics, from which women are excluded.

brainwashing

systematic indoctrination that changes or undermines one's convictions, especially political.

It may be time for a re-read of *Nineteen Eighty-Four*, *Brave New World* or *A Clockwork Orange*.

branch stacking

the arranging for a large number of one's supporters to join a branch of a political party, in order to achieve a desired preselection or policy decision.

bread and circuses

benefits or distractions provided by a government to those it governs to deflect attention from social and economic inequalities.

The phrase comes from the Latin expression *Duas tantum res anxius optat, Panem et circenses*, which translates as 'Let the restless person hope for two things only, bread and circuses', a reference by the Roman satirist Juvenal to the ways of curbing unrest among the population of ancient Rome.

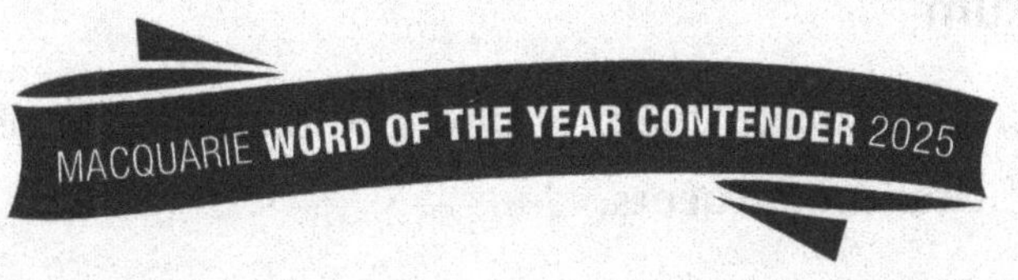

broligarchy

government by a group of wealthy men, especially those who occupy prominent roles in the technology sector.

A neat blend of **bro** and **oligarchy** wherein the **broligarchs** form a very elite **boys' club**.

The second Trump administration demonstrates the power shift in billionaire rankings from media moguls like the Murdochs to the big tech broligarchy, with Trump passing over Rupert Murdoch's recommendation for vice president (fellow billionaire Doug Burgum) for the Silicon Valley choice of JD Vance.

– *Crikey*, 31 March 2025

bung

a memo to an employee, especially of a government department, calling attention to a breach of regulations.

bunkum

insincere speech-making intended merely to please political constituents.

A US term coming from *Buncombe*, a county in the US, in North Carolina, from its Congressional representative's phrase, 'talking for Buncombe'.

Bunyip Aristocracy

the knights and dames of the Order of Australia created by Malcolm Fraser in 1976 and removed by the Labor government of Bob Hawke in 1986. More recently, the system of Australian knights and dames proposed by Tony Abbott when Prime Minister.

Aside from our knights and dames, **Bunyip Aristocracy** is used more generally to describe Australians who consider themselves to be superior to others in wealth or status.

buy back the farm

to reverse a trend towards excessive foreign ownership of companies, by means of legislation or other government control.

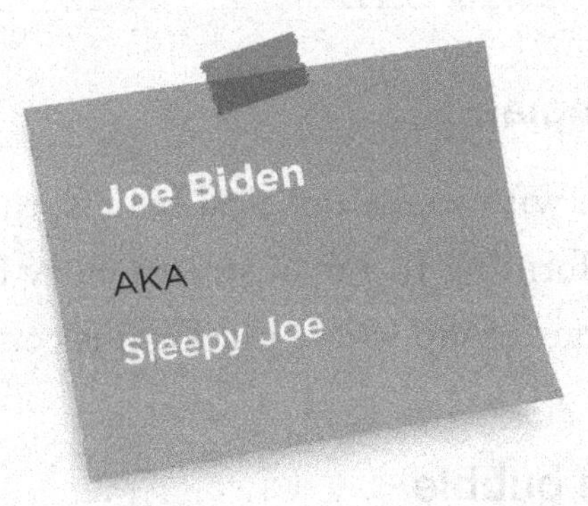

There they are, a conga line of suckholes on the conservative side of Australian politics.

Mark Latham on the Coalition
House of Representatives, Hansard, 5 February 2003

Callithumpian

a person with vague political beliefs, thought of as not conforming to a mainstream party but belonging to a minor group whose platform is confused.

Canberra bubble

a term used to describe the environment within which politicians operate, seemingly unconcerned about and unaffected by events taking place outside.

While the term had been in use for some time, Scott Morrison made regular use of it, most noticeably after he became prime minister in 2018. The term is often used to highlight how the government is seen as being disconnected from the real issues that matter to everyday Australians and to describe their trivial and petty goings-on.

Capital Hill

a nickname for Parliament House, which is also the location on which it sits.

I don't believe that government is more impressive if it is on a hill.

– *Gough Whitlam,* The Sydney Morning Herald, *17 August 1968*

captain's call

a decision made by a political or business leader without consultation with colleagues. Also, **captain's pick**.

Originally used as a cricketing term for a decision made by the captain without consultation with other members of the team.

> *Prime Minister Anthony Albanese overrode senior minister Michelle Rowland to shelve a clampdown on gambling ads and avoid a brawl with media and sports bosses ahead of the election, in his fourth captain's call aimed at shutting down controversial policies.*
>
> – *The Sydney Morning Herald*, 21 April 2025

For the first time in the history of Macquarie's Word of the Year, the public chose the same winner as the Word of the Year Committee. **Captain's call** was doubly deemed the most valuable contribution to Australian English for 2015. The term made the leap from cricket into politics to describe decisions made by Tony Abbott, who was Prime Minister at the time, that were seen to be made unilaterally, without consultation with his colleagues or cabinet. The more controversial the decision, the more attention the term received, and it quickly became embedded in the Australian lexicon. One such **captain's call** was his decision to award a knighthood to Prince Philip.

chardonnay socialist

a person with a comfortable upper middle-class income who espouses left-wing views that have no real impact on their own life.

chequebook diplomacy

the conduct of diplomatic associations at a national level by offering money in exchange for support.

Australia's **chequebook diplomacy** is primarily seen with providing economic aid, incentives or investment to our Pacific neighbours. It's also given with the quieter intention of countering China's growing influence in the region.

China hawk

a westerner who is opposed to the increasing dominance of China, especially as manifested in its territorial policies and its attempt to influence the politics of other countries.

Especially used of politicians, political advisers and commentators who hold these views. For the **China hawk's** counterpart, see **panda hugger**.

Cinderella state

a state or territory of Australia which is considered to be financially or politically disadvantaged by the federal government.

From *Cinderella*, the fairytale heroine who is taken advantage of and treated poorly. While various states have laid claim to being a Cinderella state, it is Western Australia who are most strident.

> *But the quest for the next big thing goes on. SA is Australia's Cinderella state – the one perpetually left behind – and it can't help but pine for the fairy godmother, a consequential project that will make everything right. In the real world, things are not that easy.*
>
> – *The Australian*, 6 April 2022

cleanskin

a candidate for election or an elected representative in parliament who is not formally affiliated with a political party – an independent.

This sense of **cleanskin** shares the notion of 'being

without something'. The term can also be used to describe an unbranded animal, a bottle of wine without a brand name and someone without any tattoos.

clusterfuck

an operation in which a number of things go wrong at the same time, all contributing to a disastrous situation.

Originally US military slang from the 1980s.

coal hugger

a derogatory term for a person who favours coal-fired energy production over other sources of energy.

Use of **hugger** as a word element also being applied in a derogatory manner to both the **tree hugger** and **panda hugger**.

conspiracy theory

any theory which proposes that some damaging event or situation which lacks an obvious explanation has been brought about by the unseen and evil machinations of government or covert organisations.

A US term from the early 1900s. It was originally considered a neutral term but became pejorative in the 1960s. Now often used hand in hand with other terms such as **tinfoil hats**, **cookers**, **truthers** and **QAnon**.

cooker

a not-so-nice name for a conspiracy theorist. A person who is delusional, as though under the influence of alcohol or recreational drugs.

I don't know what the credentials are to get into the cooker conspiracy club, but they would probably involve some secret handshake and a genuine disgust of science and evidence.

– David Shoebridge, Senate Hansard, 27 March 2023

coup d'état

a sudden and decisive measure in politics, especially one effecting a change of government illegally or by force.

A French term literally meaning *stroke of state*. Often used to refer to leadership spills or party coups.

1991 Paul Keating's challenge and replacement of Bob Hawke

2010 Leadership spill with Julia Gillard replacing Kevin Rudd

2013 A 'return the favour' leadership spill with Kevin Rudd ousting Julia Gillard

2015 Malcolm Turnbull's challenge and replacement of Tony Abbott

2018 Leadership spill with Scott Morrison replacing Malcolm Turnbull

cowards castle

parliament viewed as an arena in which statements that are possibly libellous can be made under protection of parliamentary privilege and therefore without fear of legal redress.

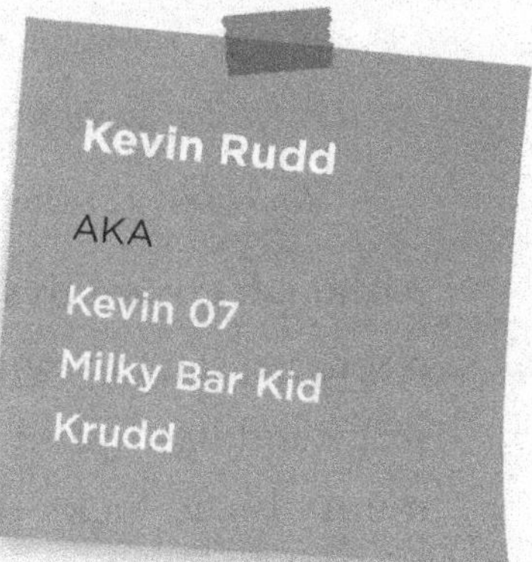

Including, but not limited to, allegations of corruption, fraud, embezzlement, immoral or dishonest behaviour.

cozzie livs

a humorous play on **cost of living**.

> *We're in the midst of a cost-of-living crisis, so it's not surprising that couples fight about money three times more than anything else, with 70 per cent admitting cozzie livs is messing not just with their relationship, but with their life milestones. From putting off family plans, to struggling to pay the rent – or a monster mortgage – financial strain is a recipe for skyrocketing stress levels.*
>
> – *Herald Sun*, 22 September 2024

Although **cozzie livs** was coined in the UK, it resonated soundly with Australians, with its **-ie** suffix and its clipped formation, reminiscent of **menty b** and **locky d**. And what could be a more Australian approach to a major social and economic problem than to treat it with a bit of humour and informality?

The pressures of **cozzie livs** played a significant factor in the 2025 federal election.

creative accounting

the structuring or adapting of accounts to meet a desired outcome, to an extent that is misleading but not illegal.

credibility gap

the difference between what is said, as by a politician, and what is actually meant or done.

The size of the **credibility gap** being judged by the court of public opinion.

crocodile tears

false or insincere tears, as the tears said to be shed by crocodiles over those they devour. Also used to mean any hypocritical show of sorrow. The term **crocodile tears** has been used to call out a politician for what the public perceive as performative behaviour, especially when their words are not backed up by their actions.

cronyism

unfair partiality shown, especially in political appointments, for one's friends.

Related to **crony capitalism**, a practice in which contracts and appointments are awarded to friends and family rather than by tender or merit.

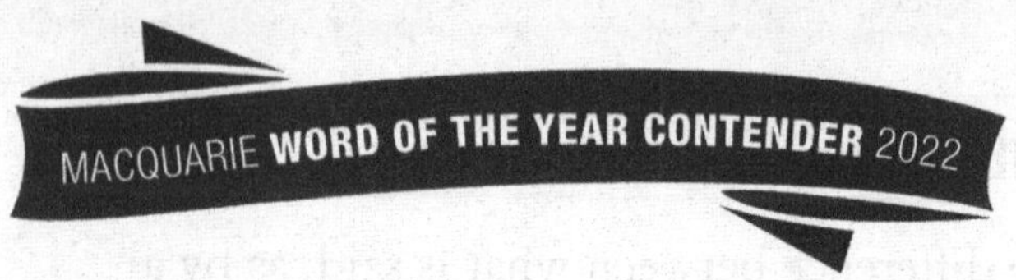

crumb maiden

a person who acts to support existing power structures which may be detrimental to their reputation or harmful to their community, in order to receive some small personal benefit or reward.

A derogatory term used especially of women in politics.

> *He [Simon Holmes à Court] complains about the "viciousness" targeting the teals while engaging in a healthy track record of bitchiness. He goes and slanders accomplished Liberal women, calling them "crumb maidens" and trashing their achievements, then sits on a panel to talk about the attitudes of Australian men.*
>
> – *The Australian*, 30 April 2025

cuck

a weak man, especially used of a man with politically progressive views.

This derogatory term comes from the shortened form of **cuckold** – the husband of an unfaithful wife.

> You want to know what political manoeuvre was used to remove me? ... I can't describe it other than to say it wiggles, it's shapely, it's cold-blooded and its name is Ainsley Gotto.
>
> – Dudley Erwin on Ainsley Gotto, The Sydney Morning Herald, 15 November 1969

What's this dipstick up to?

Barnaby Joyce on Malcolm Turnbull
Sky News, 14 November 2023

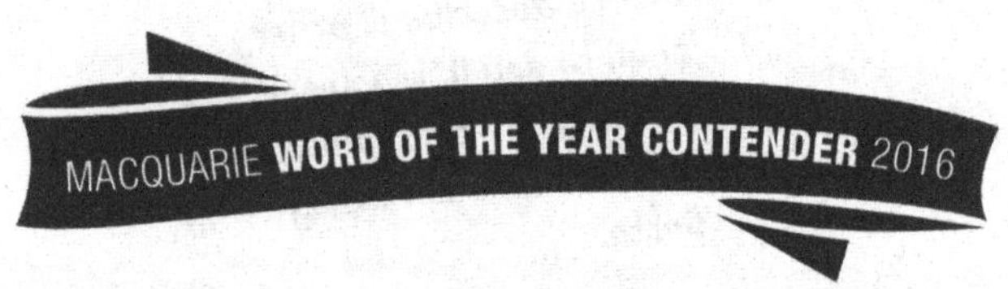

dark money

political funding given to non-profit organisations which are not required to disclose their donors, the funding channelled in this way being used to influence political outcomes beneficial to the original donors.

> *"This week the Australian Electoral Commission released the annual donations disclosures, which show more than $67 million in donations to the Labor Party, the Coalition and Greens from undeclared sources,"* Dr Haines said. *"Tens of*

millions of dollars in dark money going to the major players - including from gambling companies and others trying to influence government policy.

– Anthony Bunn, *The Border Mail*, 5 February 2025

dead cat bounce

a slight and temporary recovery in the popularity or support that a politician, political party or policy often experiences before continuing to further decline.

Originally a finance term used to describe the slight recovery that a market often experiences before relapsing into a prolonged slump. Distressingly called so from the image of a dead cat being hit by a vehicle which leaps into the air on impact as if alive, only to fall back onto the road.

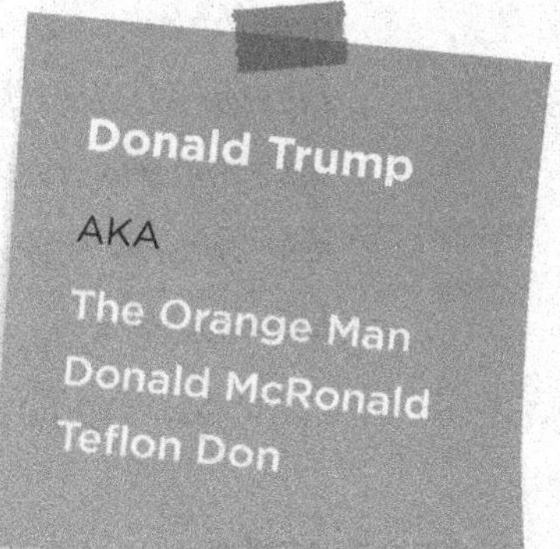

debt-trap diplomacy

a strategy, employed by a country or other institution, of lending to a foreign nation in order to increase political leverage, as by imposing conditions which the borrower is unable to fulfil, thereby forcing them to accept political or economic concessions in lieu of repayment.

> *Tonga's Chinese debt is held up by some as a prime example of what's been called China's debt-trap diplomacy in the Pacific region. Australia's Foreign Minister Julie Bishop is among those to voice concerns about the potential for unsustainable debt burdens to erode the sovereignty of Pacific Island nations.*
>
> – *ABC News*, 19 July 2018

deep state

a secret organisation alleged to exist within a state's bureaucracy, intelligence agencies and security forces, aiming to control and subvert democratic processes and institutions.

Also, **dark state.**

I know he prefers to sit in dark rooms with his little tin foil hat on and draw out his policies.

Leeane Enoch on Colin Boyce, Queensland Parliament, Record of Proceedings, 19 September 2019

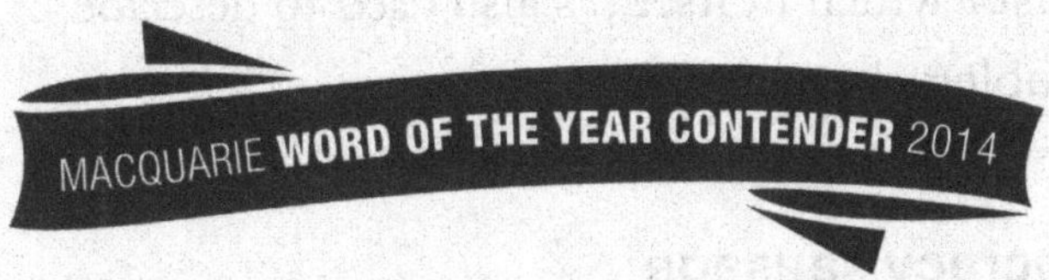

defund

to stop the flow of government funds to an organisation, enterprise, program, etc.

Defunding more frequently occurs after each change in government.

> *The Coalition has also promised to defund the Environmental Defenders Office, which has become a political football, having its funding cut under former PM Tony Abbott and then restored under the Albanese government.*
>
> – *ABC News*, 28 March 2025

demagogue

a leader who uses the passions or prejudices of the populace to further their own interests; an unprincipled popular orator or agitator.

More commonly known by the term **rabble-rouser** which in itself, is also used to describe troublemakers.

democracy sausage

a sausage sandwich which a voter can obtain at a polling booth on polling day.

Depending upon where you live in Australia, the **democracy sausage** will be variously called **sausage in bread**, **sausage sizzle** or **sausage sandwich**. A hotly contested issue.

dirt digging

research into the past life of a political candidate in order to find something discreditable about them.

From the phrase **dig the dirt on someone**.

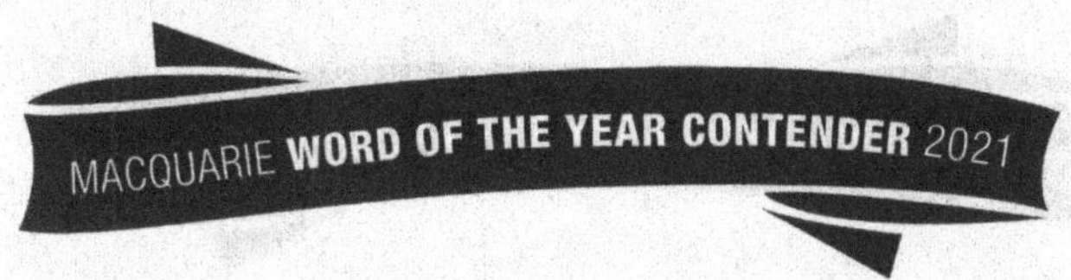

dirt file

a collection of information about a person, group, etc., which would be detrimental to the subject if revealed.

> *Simmering tensions between rival NSW Labor leadership factions boiled over on Tuesday morning after an internal dirt file on a potential leader was distributed to the media.*
>
> – *The Sydney Morning Herald*, 25 May 2021

dirty laundry

private history, especially that of a scandalous nature.

To **wash** or **air one's dirty laundry in public** is to reveal or discuss such matters from one's private life. Also, dirty linen.

dirty tricks

underhand activities designed to discredit or smear a political opponent.

disaster capitalism

the practice of taking advantage of a widespread and serious disaster, such as flood, fire, pandemic, war, etc., especially for financial gain or, of a government, to introduce privatisation, deregulation and legislation to their advantage.

> *The Victorian Labor Government's decision to lift the moratorium on onshore gas exploration is an appalling example of disaster capitalism. While the state faces a pandemic, the Government has conveniently decided to announce more gas extraction in a decision that will have far-reaching implications for decades to come.*
>
> – The Greens, 17 March 2020

do the Harry

to run away or leave promptly; to make oneself scarce.

In full, the phrase is **do the Harold Holt**, which is rhyming slang for 'bolt'. **Doing the Harry** refers to our erstwhile Prime Minister who disappeared while swimming. Holt had a swimming complex in Melbourne named after him following his disappearance and presumed drowning.

dog whistling

the making of a public statement designed to appeal to a particular group of voters while drawing no response from the rest of the electorate.

With reference to the selective signalling of a literal dog whistle. **Dog-whistle politics** simply being politics characterised by **dog whistling**.

Mr Whitlam treats the truth like a dog with a bone. He plays with it for a while and then buries it.

Malcolm Fraser, Papua New Guinea Post-Courier, *19 November 1970*

done like a dinner

completely defeated or outwitted.

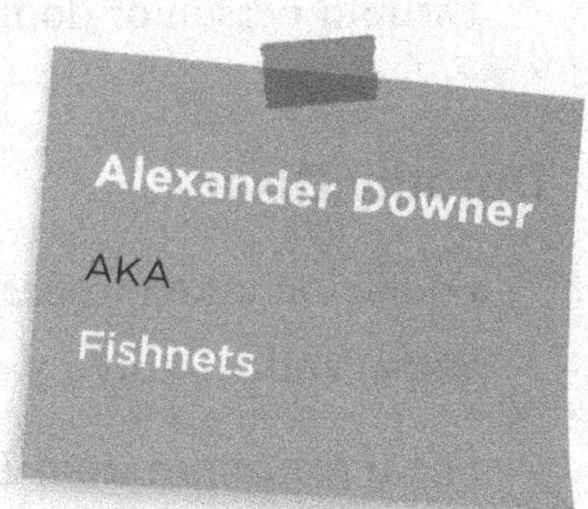

The answer is, mate, because I want to do you slowly.

Paul Keating on John Hewson, House of Representatives Hansard, 15 September 1992

dollar diplomacy

a government policy of promoting the business interests of its citizens in other countries.

donkey vote

in a compulsory preferential system of voting, a vote in which the voter's apparent order of preference among the candidates listed on the ballot paper corresponds with the order in which the names appear in the list, so that the voter is probably not expressing any preference at all.

From the idea that a voter behaving in such a way is a stupid person or donkey.

Dorothy Dixer

a question asked in parliament specifically to allow a propagandist reply by a minister.

The term comes from *Dorothy Dix*, the pen-name of American journalist Elizabeth Meriwether Gilmer,

1870–1951. She wrote a column of advice to people with emotional problems but it was thought that she wrote her more intriguing letters herself. In 2024, the Tasmanian government proposed banning such questions from their parliament.

doublespeak

convoluted language which is intended to deceive and mislead, often under a mask of technical jargon.

Doublespeak often employs **weasel words** to dilute, obscure or confuse.

doublethink

the postulated ability to accept two contradictory facts simultaneously, especially as it is assumed to be demonstrated by politicians, businesspeople, etc., in a desire not to admit to contradictions in their statements, policies, etc.

The term was coined by English writer George Orwell in his 1949 novel *Nineteen Eighty-Four*.

dove

a politician or political adviser who favours

conciliatory policies as a solution to armed conflict. The opposite of a **hawk**.

drain the swamp

to remove corruption from government, a political party, etc.

drink the Kool Aid

to accept unquestioningly an opinion, proposal, policy, explanation, etc.

An adoption of the US phrase which references the infamous Jonestown massacre, in which cult followers were given *Kool Aid*, a US brand of soft drink, laced with strychnine, to drink.

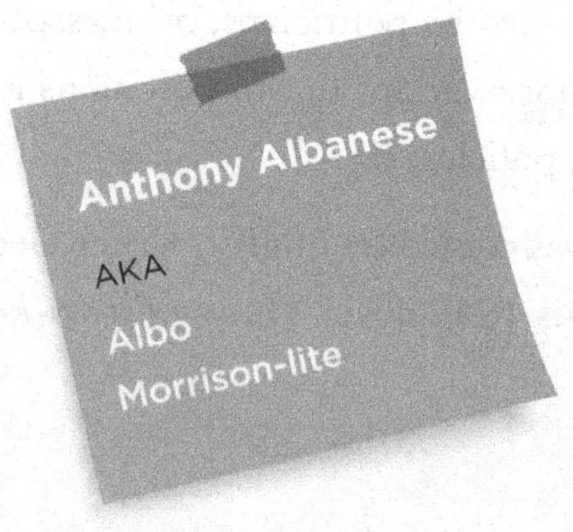

Your child will turn into a demon, if you have such evil thoughts. [. . .] Evil thoughts will make your child a demon.

Belinda Neal on Sophie Mirabella
Hansard, 28 May 2008

echo chamber

an environment where like-minded people reinforce each other's views and opinions.

Usually to the detriment of **civil discourse** which would allow open and constructive dialogue allowing differing viewpoints to be shared without disrespect.

entryism

the strategy of joining an existing political party with the intention of changing its political agenda. Also, **entrism**.

The Leader of the Opposition (Mr Peacock) is more to be pitied than despised, the poor old thing. The Liberal Party of Australia ought to put him down like a faithful old dog because he is of no use to it and of no use to the nation.

Paul Keating

House of Representatives, Hansard, 22 August 1984

faceless men

men who exercise political power without having to take personal or public responsibility for their actions.

This term was used originally by Labor detractors particularly in the 1963 Federal election campaign to refer to non-parliamentary members of the Labor Executive and their influence over elected representatives. Has been in common use ever since.

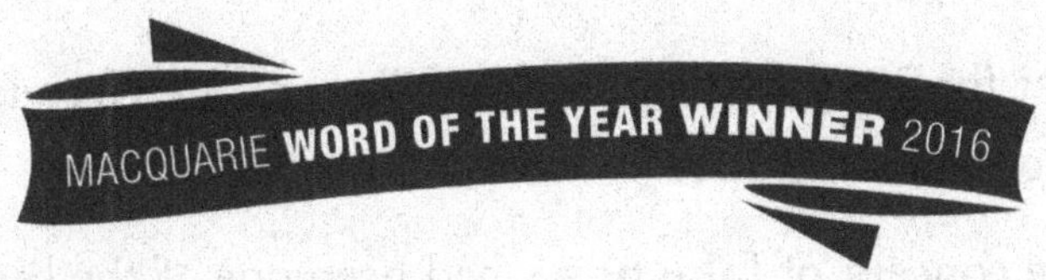

fake news

disinformation and hoaxes published on websites for political purposes or to drive web traffic, the incorrect information being passed along by social media.

Fake news quickly became used in a different way. A term used by a person, organisation, etc., to cast doubt upon information which they view as opposed or detrimental to their own, regardless of the accuracy of the information.

> *Fake news is more widespread today than ever before. Political activists who want to unfairly influence voters create false news stories. Unscrupulous media companies publish falsehoods as clickbait. Political regimes spread false propaganda to support their policies. And the blurring line between entertainment and news leads to writing that doesn't comply with journalistic standards.*
>
> – The Bronfenbrenner Center for Translational Research, *Psychology Today*, Updated April 29, 2025

Not only did **fake news** take out the Word of the

Year for 2016, it took out the Word of the Decade when held in 2021.

The concept of **fake news** had been one of the big issues of 2016, not only in Australia but around the world. While the term was around beforehand, we think of **fake news** as emblematic of Donald Trump's 2016 presidential campaign and the four years that followed it. The phenomenon became part of our lives so quickly and was so overwhelming that school courses were developed to teach children strategies for detecting **fake news**. The ease with which we have seen this term being thrown around to instantly rob something of its credibility has just gone from strength to strength. **Fake news** hit new heights in 2025 with Trump's second presidency.

false-flag attack

an attack secretly planned or carried out by a government against its own people, which is then publicly attributed to another nation in order to justify retaliatory action.

False-flag refers to the practice of pirate ships which flew false national flags in order to deceive other ships. Luckily in Australia there have only been allegations of false-flag attacks rather than confirmed actions.

fascist

anyone with extreme right-wing, sometimes racist, views.

While **facism** originally referred to certain European nationalist authoritarian regimes, it has also come to mean any extreme right-wing ideology, especially one which advocates for stronger police powers and enforcement of arbitrary laws.

feed the chooks

of a politician, to control the type and amount of information released to the media, especially by means of a press conference or press release.

The phrase was popularised by Queensland premier Sir Joh Bjelke-Petersen, who likened reporters to chickens in the way they 'scratch around' for information.

filibuster

to impede legislation by using obstructive tactics, especially by making long speeches.

While **filibustering** is not as common as it is in the US, it is very much in practice here. As of 2025, the longest filibuster is attributed to US Senator Strom Thurmond – 24 hours and 18 minutes against the Civil Rights Act of 1957.

free kick

an opportunity for a political party to achieve success in presenting its policies or points of view to the electorate, largely because of a strategic error made by the opposition.

Free kick originally came from football with the meaning 'a kick awarded to a team after an infringement by the opposing side'.

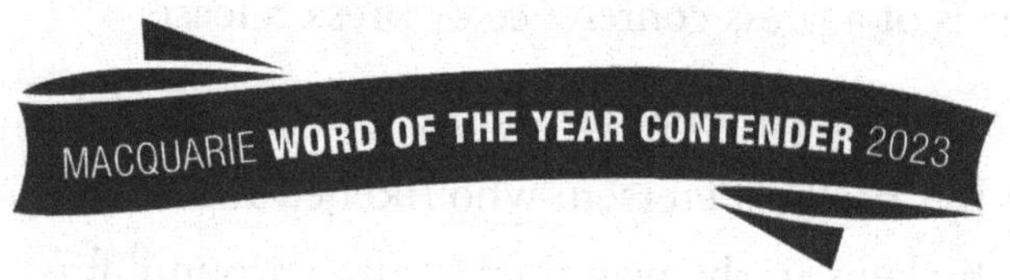

friendshoring

a government practice of redirecting supply chain networks to foreign countries who are regarded as political or economic allies. Also, **ally-shoring**.

> *Reciprocity should be a key feature of friendshoring agreements, so both parties have skin in the game and incentive to honour the deal.*
>
> – *The Australian*, 25 March 2025

front-stab

to betray someone openly, without subterfuge.

A humorous allusion to **backstab**. For when **backstabbing** is simply too much effort, or you really, really just don't care what people think. The **front-stabber** has 'more hide than Jessie'.

> *He [Scott Morrison] has to get people to believe the government is not a haven for apprentice bullies or embittered, intolerant old men. In the face of the backstabbing, the front stabbing and the personal abuse of the past few years, he needs not only to convince decent, capable women that a political career is not hazardous to their mental or physical wellbeing but men too.*
>
> – *The Australian*, 13 September 2018

G

You stupid, foul-mouthed grub.
You piece of criminal garbage.

—

Paul Keating on Wilson Tuckey
House of Representatives, Hansard, 19 February 1986

-gate

a combining element indicating a scandal, especially a political scandal.

A most useful suffix used as a modelling from **Watergate** – a political scandal during the 1972 US presidential campaign in which five people, employed by President Nixon's re-election committee, were caught breaking into the Democratic Party headquarters in Washington DC. The investigation and attempted cover-up of White House involvement causing Nixon to resign.

While every country has experience with them, **-gate** scandals and controversies in Australia include:

Iguanagate – John Della Bosca & Belinda Neal

Utegate – Kevin Rudd

Choppergate – Bronwyn Bishop

Grangegate – Barry O'Farrell

gerrymander

an arbitrary arrangement of the political divisions of an electorate, etc., made so as to give one party an unfair advantage in elections.

glass ceiling

a barrier to the progress of something, especially to the promotion of women above a certain level of executive status in an organisation in spite of their being qualified for such positions.

A shout-out to Julia Gillard, Australia's 27th prime minister. The first and only woman to date to hold the office of prime minister in Australia.

I rise to oppose the motion moved by the Leader of the Opposition, and in so doing I say to the Leader of the Opposition:

> *I will not be lectured about sexism and misogyny by this man. I will not. The government will not be lectured about sexism and misogyny by this man – not now, not ever. The Leader of the Opposition says that people who hold sexist views and who are misogynists are not appropriate for high office. Well, I hope the Leader of the Opposition has a piece of paper and he is writing out his resignation, because if he wants to know what misogyny looks like in modern Australia he does not need a motion in the House of Representatives; he needs a mirror. That is what he needs. [. . .]*
>
> *It is misogyny, sexism, every day from this Leader of the Opposition. Every day, in every way, across the time the Leader of the Opposition has sat in that chair and I have sat in this chair, that is all we have heard from him.*
>
> – Julia Gillard on Tony Abbott, *House of Representatives, Hansard*, 9 October 2012

glass cliff

the phenomenon whereby individuals who belong to groups which are not well represented in leadership positions, such as women, are more likely to be found in positions which entail a greater than usual risk of failure.

An extension of the **glass ceiling**. After the Liberal Party experienced significant losses in the 2025 federal election, Sussan Ley was voted as leader of the Liberals – their first female leader. Breaking through the **glass ceiling** only to find herself on a **glass cliff**?

gold pass

an authority issued to a person, especially a former politician, which enables the bearer to travel free of charge.

The gold-pass scheme was first introduced in 1918 and originally provided unlimited train travel to retiring parliamentarians. This was later extended to unlimited domestic air travel before being reduced to 10 free return domestic flights each year – all using the taxpayers' money. The scheme was abolished in 2017.

government stroke

the easy pace at which work is done, supposedly typical of those working for the government; originally used specifically of convict road labourers.

graft

the acquisition of gain or advantage by dishonest, unfair, or shady means, especially through the abuse of one's position or influence in politics, business, etc.

grey corruption

dishonest and unethical practices such as cronyism, nepotism, pork-barrelling, misuse of public resources, etc. Also known as **soft corruption**.

The **grey** comes from the term **grey area**, in reference to practices that are of questionable ethics. It would be **ICACable** though.

> *Supporters of political parties have never been so partisan. This goes for my fellow progressives too – budget overruns, tender irregularities, jobs for the*

> *boys, grey corruption and the inconvenient findings of independent authorities are routinely ignored if they reflect badly on "our" side.*
>
> – *Institute of Community Directors Australia*, 6 February 2024

grey power

the influence, especially political, exerted by the elderly.

gunboat diplomacy

diplomacy or foreign affairs in conjunction with the use or threat of military force.

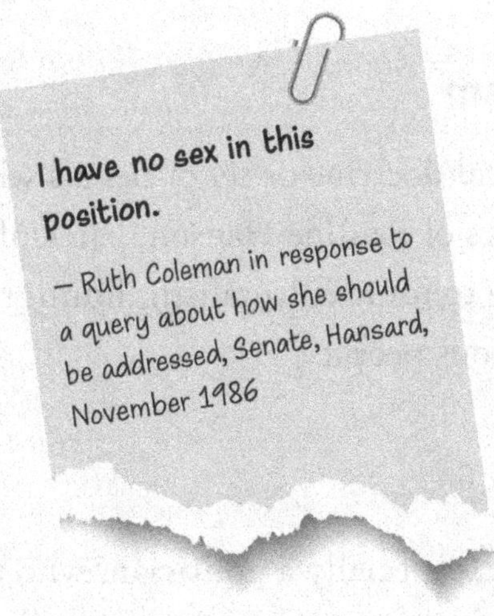

Oh, look, it's just Howard being Howard, isn't it, you know. The little desiccated coconut's under pressure and he's attacking anything he can get his hands on.

Paul Keating on John Howard
ABC Radio Sydney, 5 March 2007

Hansonism

a political doctrine or set of beliefs which incorporate the views of Pauline Hanson, particularly an adverse attitude to multiculturalism, immigration, and Indigenous people.

hardliner

a person, especially a politician, who takes an uncompromising view on an issue.

hatchet man

a person who is delegated all of the unpleasant tasks, especially those considered underhanded and unscrupulous.

hawk

a politician, political adviser, commentator, etc., who aggressively opposes the policies of a country which they consider to be not in the interests of their own country.

Hawk is also used for someone who favours aggressive or intransigent military policies. The opposite of a **dove**.

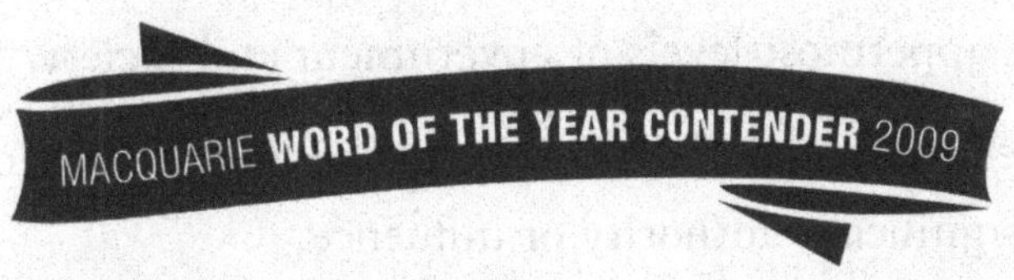

head-nodder

a supporter of a politician or other public figure who stands beside them in the frame of a television shot and nods their head in agreement with what the speaker is saying. Marketing 101.

Confoundingly, some **head-nodders** start nodding

before a word is spoken. The art of how often and how enthusiastically one should nod remains a mystery.

> *Meanwhile, poor Damian Hale, an accomplished head-nodder at press conferences, was pushed off nodding duty by the Member for Lindsay David Bradbury, who stood behind the PM at her Darwin event.*
>
> – *Northern Territory News*, 11 July 2010

headhunting

the elimination of political enemies.

high places

the uppermost levels of government and society. Used metaphorically to refer to those with positions of significant authority or influence.

hip-pocket nerve

an imaginary nerve which is sensitive to demands for one's money, especially through government action to increase taxation or weaken one's economic security.

hired gun

a person who is employed to deal with any opposition to the plans of a government, organisation, etc., and whose role it is to determine strategy and resolve disputes.

hold the hand out

to demand bribe money.

The phrase can also be used of the public to mean to exploit the benefits given out by the government and other welfare organisations. Bribing on one hand, exploiting on the other.

hollow log

a government body such as a statutory authority which is able to keep funds in reserve rather than lose them into general revenue.

Hollow log can also be used to more generally mean an unnoticed or secret fund of money.

hollow man

someone who is perceived as lacking in morals, values, substance, etc., and who acts in one's self-interest.

Famously from the poem *The Hollow Men* (1925) by TS Eliot, which describes a world inhabited by empty and spiritually dead people.

hospital pass

the passing on of a difficult undertaking to someone else.

Hospital pass is another term that has come across from the world of football. There it refers to a pass given to a player who will inevitably be heavily tackled on receiving the ball.

hospital vote

the vote from electors in hospitals, nursing homes, etc., who are visited by electoral officials to take their ballot on the day, or who cast a pre-poll vote.

hot potato

Commonly used in the phrase to **play hot potato** – to pass the responsibility or blame for something from one person to another. Otherwise known as **passing the buck.**

I

Well, the thing about poor old Costello,
he's all tip and no iceberg, you know.

Paul Keating on Peter Costello, ABC News, 2007

ICACable

a term used to describe the actions, behaviour, negotiations, etc., of a politician or public servant, which is deemed to be worthy of scrutiny by the NSW or SA Independent Commission Against Corruption (ICAC).

Former NSW MP Daryl Maguire has conceded that his desperate campaign to secure a "tickle from up top" by sharing Gladys Berejiklian's

> *email address with a "pissed off" Louise Waterhouse was an "ICAC-able" offence.*
>
> – *Weekend Australian*, 17 October 2020

Although Victoria has a similar corruption body IBAC, and Queensland and Western Australia with CCCs, ICAC appears to be the only one to have '**-abled**' itself into our lexicon.

in the wilderness

out of political office.

inside the tent

numbered among those considered to be allied in their interests, world view, etc.

From a phrase coined by US president Lyndon B Johnson '*it's better having them inside the tent pissing out than outside the tent pissing in*'.

J

He turns away! If ever there was a shiver waiting for a spine to run up, it is his.

—

Malcolm Turnbull on Brendan O'Connor
House of Representatives, Hansard, 29 March 2017

jeff

to downsize, reduce funding to or close down an institution, government department, etc. To retrench or dismiss. Or to ruin or destroy in a heartless and unfair way.

You couldn't lie straight in bed.

— Peter Dutton on Anthony Albanese, 9 News, 2025 Debate

A term in use in Victoria. **Jeff** being an abbreviation of Jeffrey Kennett, premier of Victoria 1992–99, who reduced government spending dramatically. *Our hopes of getting a fair wage deal have been jeffed.* Occasionally people have used ***Kennett*** in the same way.

jobs for the boys

appointments of friends or supporters to office made by those in power.

See boys' club.

The harsh realities of government proved too great a hurdle for a Labor Party which had spent so many long and bitter years in opposition. Too many of the men who became ministers in that government were too old, too stupid and too embittered from their long walk in the wilderness.

Graham Richardson, Quarterly Essay 8, Groundswell, November 2002

I think it must be said of him that he is an interesting physical phenomenon. He is the only man I know of whom it can be said that his Achilles heel is in his mouth.

Sir James Killen on Gough Whitlam
House of Representatives, Hansard, 2 March 1972

kakistocracy

government by the worst or least qualified people in the state.

kangaroo ticket

a presidential ticket where the nominated vice-president has more appeal to the voters than the presidential candidate.

A US term from the notion that a kangaroo has more weight and power in its back legs than in its forelimbs.

kitchen cabinet

a group of chosen advisers to a prime minister or premier, perceived to have more influence than the official cabinet.

knife

to endeavour to defeat in a secret or underhand way.

Essential if engaging in a spot of backstabbing. To **knife someone in the back** is to betray someone, especially to destroy their reputation or career in their absence.

know where the bodies are buried

to know all the scandals and secrets of the past.

koala diplomacy

diplomacy between Australia and other countries, facilitated by interactions and photo opportunities with koalas and foreign dignitaries or other prominent figures.

Similar to the longer practised **panda diplomacy**.

L

It was the limpest performance I have ever seen.
It was like being flogged with a warm lettuce.
It was like being mauled by a dead sheep.

Paul Keating on John Hewson
House of Representatives, Hansard, 31 October 1989

laberal

of or relating to the two major political parties of Australia, viewed collectively as holding views, policies, etc., which are not dissimilar.

A blend of **Labor** and **Liberal, laberal** can also be upper case. Interestingly, **laberal** is preferred over the reverse portmanteau of **libor**.

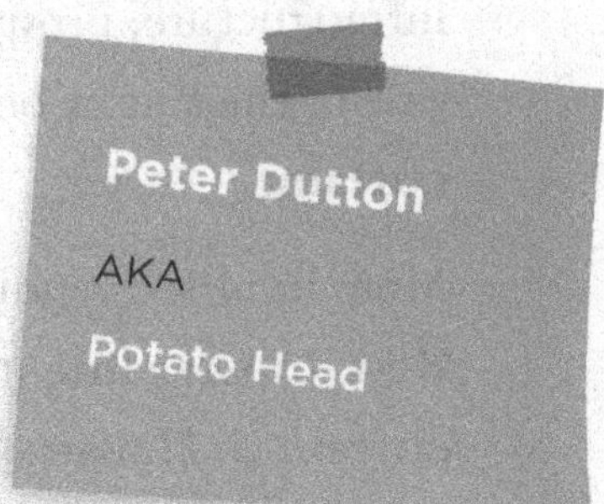

lame duck

a public official or elected office holder who is weakened in power or authority, as one approaching the end of their term of office.

lapdog

a person who, through admiration for or infatuation with a superior, unthinkingly endorses their every act.

latte line

an imaginary line supposedly marking a socio-economic and cultural division, with people living on one side having greater access to jobs, infrastructure, prosperity, etc., and those on the other side of the line as being disadvantaged. Also, **quinoa curtain.**

More localised renditions of the **latte line** are the **Red Rooster line** in Sydney and the **flannelette curtain** in Hobart. Wider NSW also has the

sandstone curtain of the Great Dividing Range. Here, the mountains are regarded as dividing the people who live along the east coast from the inhabitants of rural and regional NSW, the former perceived as being the recipients of large amounts of government spending and the latter as being overlooked by the government.

> *Largely spanning Sydney's north-eastern suburbs, the schools above the Latte Line are responsible for producing the bulk of the highest HSC results, when compared with the areas below the Latte Line in the southwest.*
>
> – *Education Today*, Term 1 2017

lemon socialism

a pejorative term for the provision of government financial assistance to a private company of a size or type which makes it significant to the country's economy, in order to prevent the collapse of the company and subsequent negative impact on the economy as a whole.

Lemon, in reference to a product, especially a motor vehicle, which is faulty in some way, usually characterised by unreliable and unsatisfactory performance.

locky d

lockdown imposed by a government, resulting from COVID-19.

log cabin story

an account of triumph over poverty and other hardships, intended to arouse the admiration of others, especially in politics.

loony left

a derogatory term for extreme left-wing politicians and their supporters.

lower than a snake's belly

unprincipled, despicable, contemptible.

The image of a snake is commonly used to malign someone within chambers. And while there's nothing **lower than a snake's belly**, one must be wary of all of the **snakes in the grass** that lie in wait. The quickest way to tar someone as unhinged or denigrate, is to bandy the phrase **mad as a cut snake**.

lunar right

a derogatory term for extreme right-wing politicians and their supporters. Also, **loony right**.

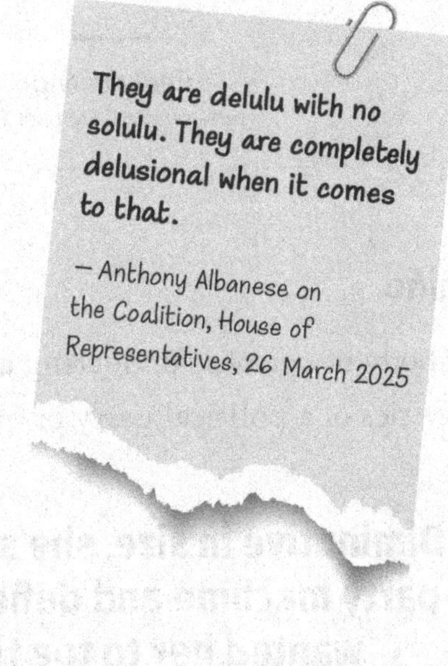

He attacks Kevin Rudd and Tony Abbott as ghosts, yet if you needed to know what Malcolm Turnbull truly believes in, what he would die in a ditch over, you would need a microscope to help you find it.

Paul Keating
news.com.au, 3 October 2018

machine

the body of persons conducting and controlling the activities of a political party or other organisation.

Diminutive in size, she stared down a party machine and defied those who wanted her to toe the line.

– ABC News on Fatima Payman crossing the floor, 26 June 2024

machine politics

politics governed by a party machine rather than by the elected politicians themselves.

malversation

improper or corrupt behaviour in office.

Malversation comes from the Latin term *male versārī* with the meaning 'behave wrongly'.

Mediscare

a campaign that fuelled fears about cuts to Medicare or privatisation of the service. A highly effective **scare campaign** of 2016.

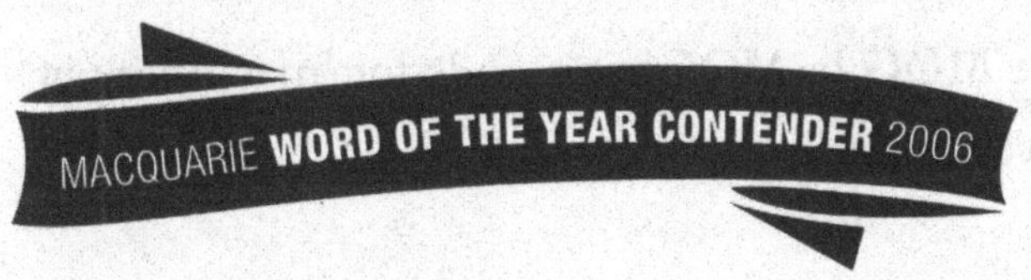

megaphone diplomacy

the diplomatic strategy of talking freely in public forums about an issue in order to persuade people to accept a particular point of view.

Albanese at first said he would not engage in

> *megaphone diplomacy, but he became more vocal over time as Assange remained locked up at Belmarsh prison in London.*
>
> – *WA Today*, 25 June 2024

minder

someone whose occupation is to protect another person, especially a politician, from doing or saying anything politically detrimental.

MOGing

the process involved in transferring staff and all associated costs, documents, etc., from one department to another under new arrangements as determined by an incoming government.

The **MOG** in **MOGing** stands for 'machinery of government'.

Mr Clean

a person of impeccable morals and untarnished reputation, especially a politician regarded as never having been corrupt.

From the name of a household cleaning product

which became widely popular due in part to its advertising campaign which featured a bald but muscular character – **Mr Clean**.

muckrake

to attempt to uncover information that will discredit someone, particularly someone in public life for whom such revelations would be damaging.

The **muckraker** engaged in a spot of **mudraking** in order to **mudsling**.

mudslinging

the act of discrediting political opponents, particularly those in public office, by accusing them of misdemeanours in their public or private life.

mugwump

a US term for someone who acts as an independent or affects superiority, especially in politics.

That is a bit rich coming from this opposition led by a man who Peter Costello said you could not trust with the economy, by a man who his former boss John Hewson said was innumerate, by somebody who thinks that the NBN is just for video games, by someone who opposes everything in this place and stands for nothing. He is the Nancy Reagan of Australian politics without the astrology – say no to everything, just rancid, dripping, relentless negativity.

Jason Clare on Tony Abbott
House of Representatives, Hansard, 28 February 2012

nanny state

a country or region with a government which is viewed as over-protective and inclined to excessive regulation.

narrowcast

to transmit a political message to individuals or groups in society who have previously shown support for the politician, party, etc.

non-core promise

a promise made by a political party to an electorate in the course of an election campaign, which at a later date, when in government, it deems to be peripheral to its main platform and therefore expendable.

A term attributed to prime minister John Howard in response to the accusation made soon after his winning the 1996 election that he had broken an election promise.

nothingburger

a person or thing of no consequence, influence or value, especially one of which high expectations were originally held.

While chiefly used throughout the US, **nothingburger** has been picking up traction here as a means to insult and humiliate.

Nationals senator Matt Canavan said COP26 was a "big nothingburger" and the Coalition should take on the "activist green lobby" instead of "paying lip service to it".

– *The Sydney Morning Herald*, 14 November 2021

nothing to see here

an expression used ironically to convey that, although an authority, such as the government or a government agency, would like us to believe that there is no problem, there is indeed a big problem. From the phrase used by police to move a crowd along from an incident or crime scene, **move along, nothing to see here.**

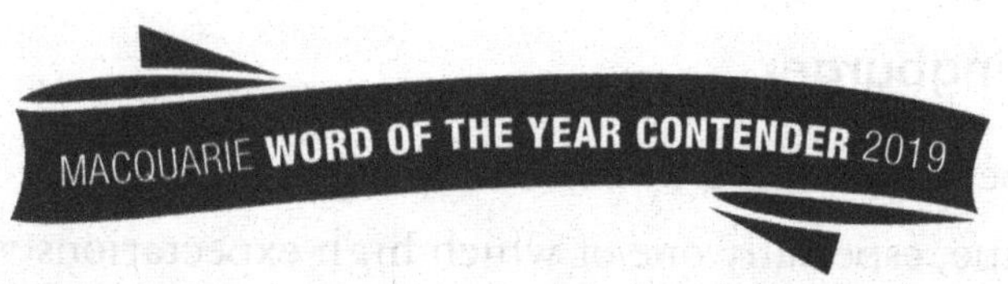

nudge unit

an organised body, especially of government, which devises interventions based on behavioural science to persuade citizens to do what they consider to be desirable or beneficial.

Nudge unit comes from the term **nudge theory** – a theory of how to effect beneficial social change by offering positive reinforcement and suggestions rather than explicit instructions, legal enforcement, etc. From a book *Nudge* published in 2008 by behavioural economists.

> *At Westmead Hospital, the nudge unit helped increase the number of emergency in-patients who use their private health insurance by two percentage points.*
>
> – *The Mandarin*, 22 July 2014

numbers man

a politician whose task is to keep track of votes, sometimes exerting influence on others to persuade them to vote as required.

All the open, empty spaces in this country are not in the outback. A lot of them are between the ears of Ministers of the Fraser Government.

Bill Hayden

House of Representatives, Hansard, 21 September 1982

oncer

a parliamentarian who has won a marginal seat in a landslide election and is likely to be voted out at the next election.

There is a trap for the Labor critics and his political opponents who have judged Anthony Albanese to be a oncer and an easy beat 'worse than Whitlam'.

– *The Australian, 26 April 2025*

Overton window

the range of ideas politically acceptable to the public which can be manipulated by organising the presentation of extreme views, either to the right or the left of centre, shifting the window's position in relation to them.

Named after Joseph Overton, 1960–2003, US political commentator.

The honourable member has been in so many parties, he is a complete political harlot.

Paul Keating on Steele Hall
House of Representatives, Hansard, 8 March 1984

panda bashing

a derogatory term for criticism of a Chinese government policy, action, etc., by another country, especially a Western country.

A person who engages in **panda bashing** being a **panda basher**. The **panda** being a widely recognised symbol of China.

An international row has erupted as the Australian prime minister, Scott Morrison, backed calls for an investigation of the origins and spread of the novel coronavirus. The Chinese government has responded by blasting out belittling messages about "panda bashing" and "victim blaming" by Australia.

– *The Guardian*, 29 April 2020

panda diplomacy

diplomacy between China and other countries, facilitated by the gift of a panda.

Compare **koala diplomacy**.

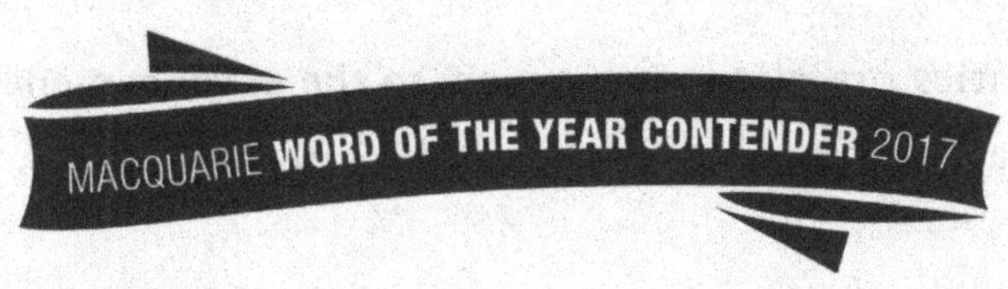

panda hugger

a derogatory term for a westerner who admires Chinese culture, in particular one who supports Chinese government policies.

Contrasting with the **panda basher**, the **panda hugger** engages in **panda hugging**. Use of **hugger** as a word element also being applied in a derogatory manner to both the **tree hugger** and **coal hugger**.

> *A lot of Asian governments and opinion leaders suspect that at heart Turnbull is a panda hugger, someone who gives an excessive deference to whatever Beijing wants.*
>
> – *The Australian*, 23 June 2016

party man

a man whose actions, words, and associations are almost entirely directed or dictated by party considerations.

party politics

politics practised with a view to the advancement of a party rather than in the public interest.

pass the buck

to shift the responsibility or blame to another person.

Any person will do. Similar in intent to the **hospital pass** and **hot potato** and very much in opposition to what should be the case in **the buck stops here**. **The buck stops** here being coined by Harry

Truman, US president 1945–53.

John Howard

AKA

Little Johnny
Honest John

payola

a bribe, especially for the promotion of a commercial product through the abuse of one's position or influence.

performative activism

a derogatory term for a form of virtue signalling by a public figure, company, government, etc., which shows support for a cause in a way that requires little effort.

The **performative activist** being a public facing figure while the **social justice warrior** (SJW) also includes the everyday person.

personality cult

excessive adulation of an individual, especially a political leader.

pink

often upper case, a person with moderately left-wing or radical political opinions.

In the direction of, but not quite in, **red** territory.

pink recession

a recession or economic downturn in which women are more adversely affected than men, especially in terms of unemployment. Other terms for this are **pink-collar recession** and **she-cession**.

So called **pink** from the association of the colour with the female gender.

> *Leading Australian businesswomen have slammed the Coalition's budget for failing to support women during a "pink recession", saying its lack of funding for childcare and focus on stimulus for sectors dominated by men leaves female workers behind.*
>
> – *Australian Financial Review*, 7 October 2020

plausible deniability

a carefully crafted situation in which a member of government can safely deny any direct or exact knowledge of, and therefore any association with, any illegal or unpopular activity carried out by servants of the government, in the event that these activities become public.

While not in any way plausible, mass governmental deniability was evidenced throughout the National Anti-Corruption Commission's investigation into the Robodebt scheme.

poke the dragon

to engage in behaviour or rhetoric which may provoke a negative reaction from the government of China.

political football

an issue or project of social importance used as a means to gain a political advantage, especially by opposing political parties.

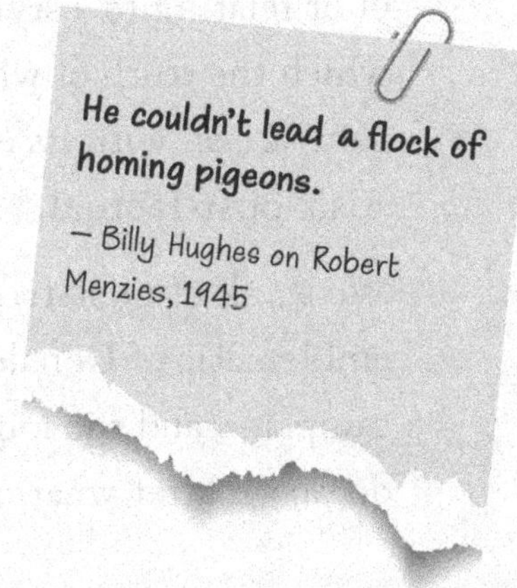

political hack

a politician who pursues the narrow goal of ensuring that their party is in power, often using methods that are to do with the exercise of power or the pursuit of expediency.

pork-barrelling

the practice of supplying an inappropriate share of government money to a person, company, institution, etc., in return for political support.

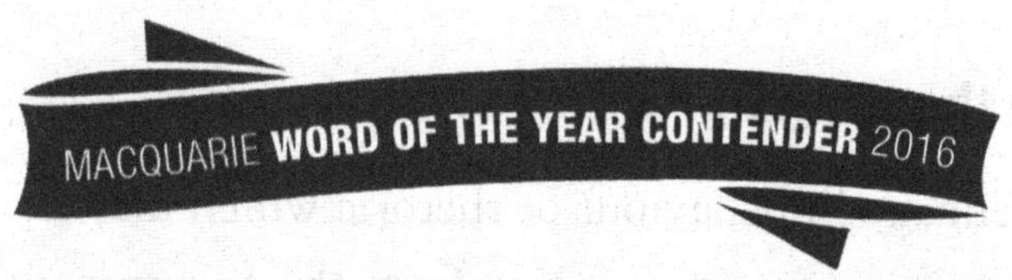

post-truth

of or relating to a style of political debate in which the truth of what is said is unimportant by comparison with its emotional appeal to the voters. Also, **post-factual**.

We think of **post-truth** like **fake news** – emblematic of Donald Trump's 2016 presidential campaign and the four years that followed it. It doesn't matter what or how many fact-checking

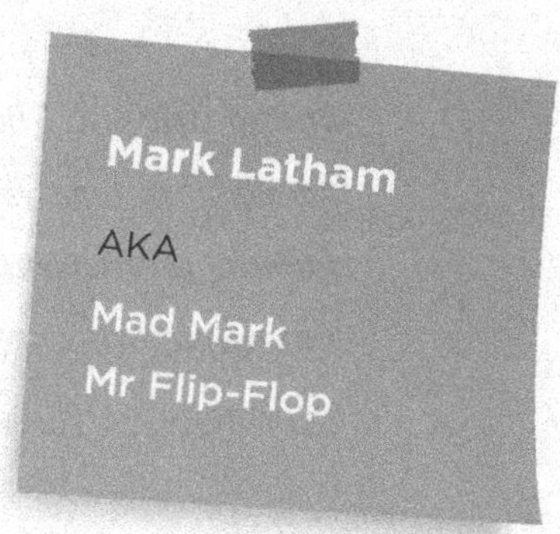

mechanisms are in place, for many, emotional appeal trumps truth. Evidenced in 2025 with Trump's second presidency.

> *Welcome to Australia's first fully fledged post-truth election campaign, where hypocrisy and deception are assets, not liabilities. A claim doesn't need verification; it just needs to sound plausible*
>
> – *The Australian*, 28 April 2025

precariat

a social class comprising people whose lives lack security and predictability, particularly in relation to jobs, income and material wellbeing.

A neat portmanteau of **precarious** and **proletariat**.

> *Accounting for 13 per cent of the sample, the precariat comprises Australia's most poverty-*

> *affected citizens. They have the lowest mean household income, many are unemployed or claiming government aid and their social and cultural capital scores are the lowest.*
>
> – *ABC News*, 24 January 2018

preference whisperer

a person who can do deals with other candidates in an election to secure preferences for their own candidate.

Just like the horse whisperer, the **preference whisperer** is well versed in dealings with intractable subjects.

press the flesh

to shake hands and talk with members of the public, as when campaigning for election, etc.

Can be taken to a new level with a spot of **baby kissing.**

pub test

the notional measure of public opinion on a proposal, candidate, etc., arrived at by asking the average drinker in a hotel what they think.

If something **passes the pub test**, it means one accepts it as reasonable and fair. If it doesn't, then pollies should beware.

puppet state

a state whose government is more or less controlled by a more powerful state.

puppetmaster

a person who manipulates others, especially in politics.

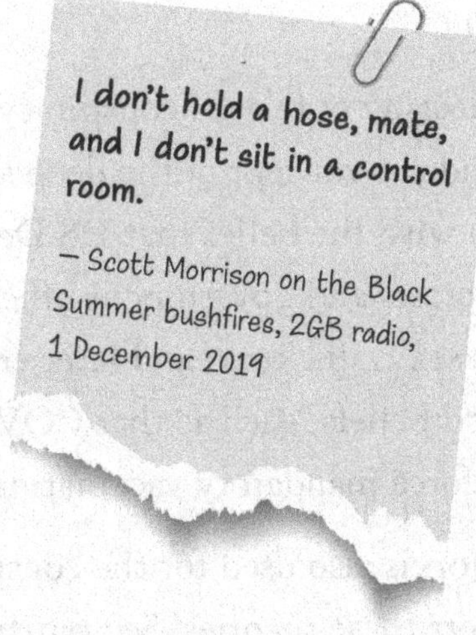

(He is a) shallow, cynical, immodest, mealy-mouthed, duplicitous, a boy in a bubble, a foreign policy imposter and unfit to lead the nation.

—

Alexander Downer on Kevin Rudd
The Australian, 11 July 2007

QAnon

a collection of related conspiracy theories revolving around the concept of the deep state, originating in 2016 with the belief that US Democrat politicians, supporters and government officials were engaged in child sex trafficking, and later encompassing various related beliefs, such as that COVID-19 is a pretence to enforce mandatory vaccination.

QAnon is also used for the conspiracy theorists who support these theories. See **truther**. Named after an anonymous internet user who signed off on their comments as Q, from **Q clearance**, the highest level of security clearance in the US Nuclear Regulatory Commission + **anon(ymous)**.

Quexit

the movement for the state of Queensland to secede from the Australian Federation.

A blend of **Queensland** and **exit**. Modelled on **Grexit**, **Brexit** and **WAxit**.

quiet majority

another name for the **silent majority**.

Made up of **quiet Australians** who are considered reserved and not vocal but who can exercise influence on election outcomes through their votes.

quinoa curtain

an imaginary line supposedly marking a socio-economic and cultural division, with people living on one side having greater access to jobs, infrastructure, prosperity, etc., and those on the other side of the line as being disadvantaged. Also, **latte line**.

I suppose that the honourable gentleman's hair, like his intellect, will recede into the darkness.

Paul Keating on Andrew Peacock
House of Representatives, Hansard, 31 May 1984

radical

someone who holds or follows extreme principles, especially left-wing political principles; an extremist.

rat

someone who quits a political party, and in particular, someone who then forms or joins another party.

Notable Australian **rats** include Billy Hughes, Joe Lyons, Vince Gair, Don Chipp, Cheryl Kernot, Cory Bernardi and Mark Latham.

ratfuck

to sabotage the political ambitions of an opponent by attempting to damage their reputation, and so ultimately to destroy their prospects of gaining power.

This term was first associated with campaigners for US president Richard Nixon's re-election in 1972. The sabotage being carried out by so called **ratfuckers**.

> *An exhausted Rudd fumed about being 'ratfucked' by China in trying to get a deal on what he'd told Australians was 'the greatest moral, economic and social challenge of our time.'*
>
> – *ASPI The Strategist*, 16 November 2015

razor gang

a government committee which reviews all expenditure with the aim of cutting back wherever possible.

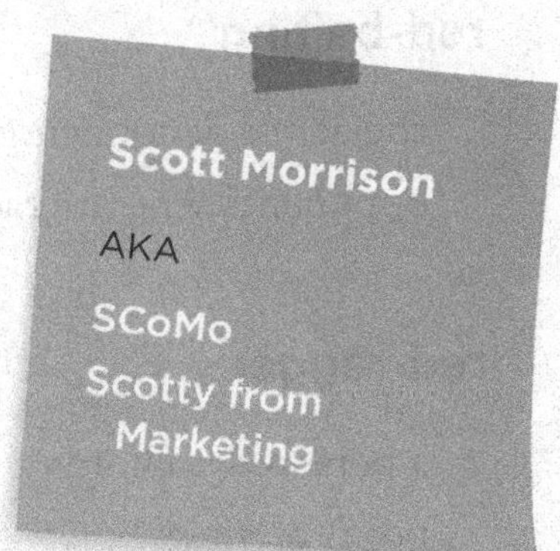

red

often upper case, an ultraradical in politics, especially a communist.

Compare **pink** and **white**.

red pill

a term used to refer to a belief or ideology which one believes everybody should share, especially of politics, anti-feminism, etc.

'*Go on, take the **red pill***'. With reference to a scene in the film *The Matrix* (1999), in which the protagonist is offered the choice between taking a **red pill** that will reveal reality's true nature and a **blue pill** that will restore his existing perceptions.

red-baiting

the act of denouncing or deprecating political opponents who are radical or left-wing.

red-ragger

a person who holds a communist or socialist political point of view.

religious right

the section of the populace which is right-wing in its political leanings with a conservatism related to a religious background.

retail politics

political strategies of the traditional kind, such as hand-shaking, baby-kissing, etc., which target an individual voter, as opposed to those such as television campaigns, newspaper advertisements, etc., which target a wide audience.

Much cheaper than **wholesale politics**.

robocall

an automated phone call using an autodialler to select phone numbers and deliver a computerised prerecorded message in electioneering.

While **robocalling** is still very much around, some campaigners show a preference for **robotexting**, as evidenced in the 2025 federal elections where we saw the Trumpet of Patriots spamming millions of voters with unsolicited texts.

robodebt

a debt owed to the government by a present or past welfare recipient, arising from an overpayment of benefits calculated by an automated process which compares the recipient's income as stated by them to the government with their income as recorded by the taxation authority, a notice of discrepancy being automatically generated.

> *"This scheme is no more likely to be fair and accurate on dead Australians as living ones," they said. "Since July 2016, Australians hit with an inaccurate robodebt have then had it reduced 65,813 times, and completely overturned 168,284 times. This government has all the ethics of a graverobber.*
>
> *"There is no low to which they won't stoop in the pursuit of a dollar. And now we know robodebt won't even allow deceased Australians to rest in peace."*
>
> – *The Australian*, 2019

An unlawful program implemented under the

Liberal government in 2016. Despite going under several official governmental names, it quickly and widely became known as the **Robodebt Scheme**, with the debts themselves **robodebts**. The program faced numerous legal challenges, and in 2020, the government settled a class-action lawsuit to the amount of $1.8 billion. In 2022 a Royal Commission was established to investigate the implementation and effects of the scheme, which further highlighted its failures and governance issues. The impacts on the physical and mental health of debt notice recipients were immense. The fact that it was voted the Word of the Year by the public in 2019 demonstrates its national impact.

roll over

of a politician, to resign gracefully.

rort

a scheme which manipulates the law or any set of regulations to gain a wrongful advantage.

rubber chicken circuit

a round of official dinners which a politician is obliged to attend.

So called from the fact that chicken is often served at such dinners, typically having been kept warm or reheated until its texture is rubbery.

rubberstamp

to give approval without consideration.

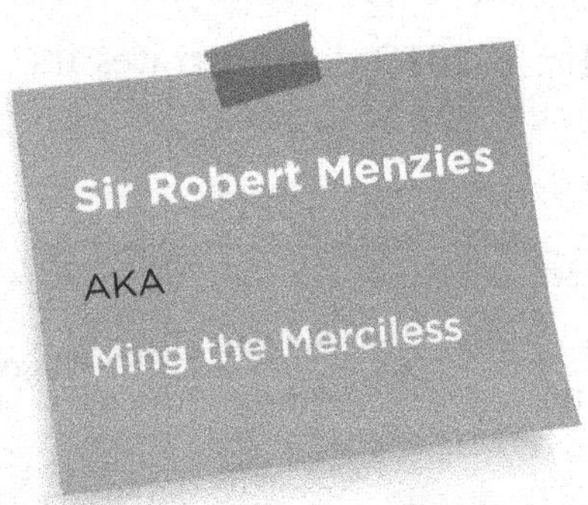

S

No one, however smart, however well educated, however experienced, is the suppository of all wisdom.

Tony Abbott
12 August 2013

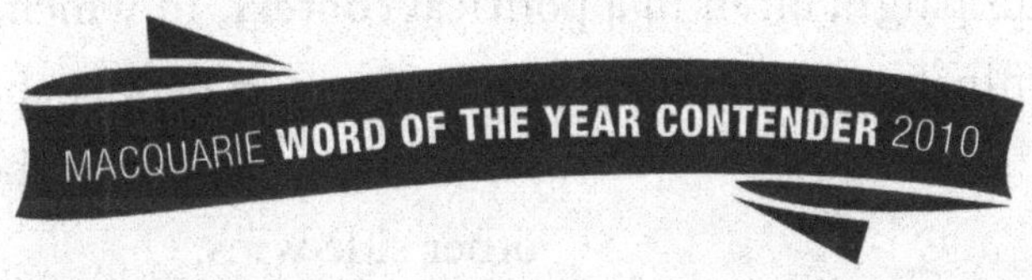

sandbagging

the attempt to secure a particular electorate against a feared swing in the vote by making election promises targeted at that electorate.

> *Labor is sandbagging its key Queensland marginal seats with a range of targeted promises, in a bid to defend its most shaky electoral gains.*
>
> – *The Courier-Mail*, 12 August 2010

sanewashing

the practice of making something that would be perceived as utterly senseless or extreme appear much more reasonable than it is, especially in politics.

While one politician trumps **sanewashing** in the news cycles, the term has been used by people on every side of politics in condemnation of their opponent's practice of presenting perceived radical or potentially dangerous ideas as if they were reasonable.

scare campaign

a campaign, often in a political context, in which the dominant strategy is to arouse alarm in people about what might happen if the other side wins.

Yes, he is Gina Rinehart's butler...

– Julia Gillard on Tony Abbott, House of Representatives, 28 May 2012

The term **Mediscare** being successfully used during the 2016 federal election and one that keeps being revisited.

shit sheet

a newsletter, flyer, blog, etc., which is a vehicle for gossip, negative or false information about people or organisations, especially those in politics.

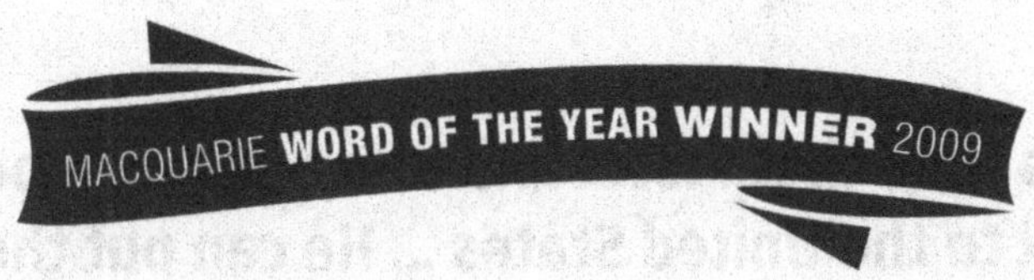

shovel-ready

(of a building or infrastructure project) capable of being initiated immediately as soon as funding is assured.

This is a favourite of politicians and often leveraged in order to demonstrate their readiness to act swiftly, stimulate the economy, create jobs and provide projects which benefit the community. As to whether they actually come about or come in on budget is quite another story.

> *Mr Katter welcomed more than $100m in vital road upgrades for his electorate but said there were other shovel ready infrastructure projects that must start immediately to take Australia out of the pandemic depression.*
>
> – *North West Star*, 23 June 2020

show pony

a person who is capable of a smooth and polished performance but who lacks any real substance.

Often media savvy and public relations focused, a show pony typically has some rizz.

It's time that Pistol and Boo buggered off back to the United States ... He can put them on the same chartered jet he flew out on to fly them back out of our nation.

– Barnaby Joyce on Johnny Depp's unauthorised entry of dogs, May 2015

silent majority

the people within a community who are not active politically and who do not express their views publicly, presumed to be numerous and to support moderate or conservative policies. Also, the **quiet majority**.

Made up of **quiet Australians**.

sing from the same songbook (or song sheet)

to speak in a similar way, supporting the same ideas, goals, aspirations, etc.

sit on (or upon)

to prevent a document from becoming public knowledge so as to avoid the action demanded by it.

Nothing to see here!

skulduggery

dishonourable proceedings; mean dishonesty or trickery. Also, **skullduggery**.

slopaganda

AI-generated, low-quality content spread to manipulate beliefs for political purposes.

A neat portmanteau of **slop** and **propaganda**.

small-l liberal

a supporter of classical liberalism, regardless of whether they are a member of the Liberal Party.

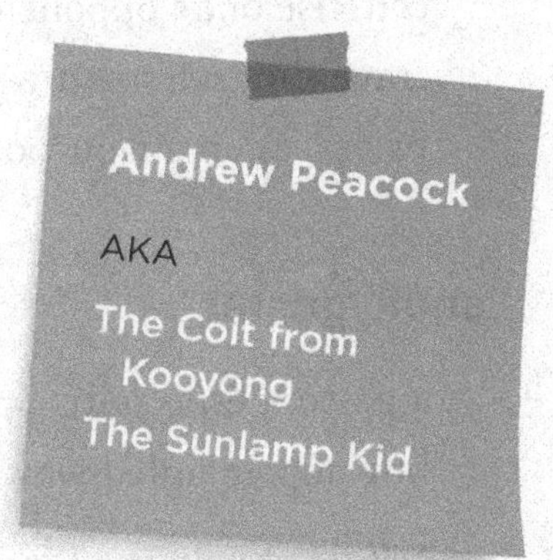

smear campaign

an organised effort to ruin a person by vilification, as by means of newspaper articles.

snake in the grass

a deceitful or treacherous person; a hidden enemy.

If one engages in such deceit and treachery they can be described as being **lower than a snake's belly**.

snake-oil salesman

a swindler or confidence trickster.

This term is used to describe politicians who are perceived as deceptive or selling false promises – inclusive of **non-core promises**. Commonly used to criticise one's opponent. From the stereotype of the travelling salesman who sold *snake oil* at exorbitant prices, as an all-purpose remedy.

snollygoster

a person, especially a politician, who acts in a shrewd but unprincipled way.

While chiefly used in the US, **snollygoster** is simply too much fun not to adopt Down Under.

snowflake

a derogatory term for a person with liberal views, regarded by conservatives as being over-sensitive; bleeding heart.

Snowflake is also used more generally for any easily offended or sensitive person. There's even the **snowflake generation** – the generation of people born in the last two decades of the 20th century. This charming appellation is from the notion that they lack substance, being overly sensitive, easily offended and easily discouraged.

social bandaid

a superficial attempt, usually by a government, to solve a social problem. See **bandaid solution**.

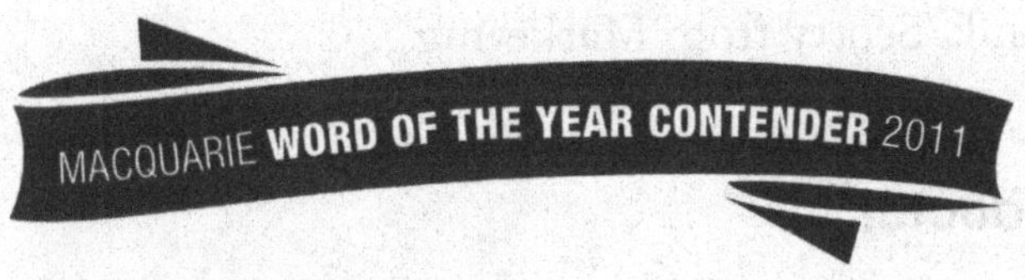

soy cap intelligentsia

a derogatory term for a class or group of persons with a comfortable upper middle-class income who espouse left-wing views that have no real impact on their own lives.

From the supposed tendency, regarded as pretentious, of such people to drink soy caps – cappuccinos made with soy milk. Very similar in nature to the **chardonnay socialists.**

> *And the new slogan for the state need not only affect our number plates, it could define us as Victorians. It could be something that encompasses the soy cap intelligentsia with the flood and drought-ridden farmer, multiculturalism with the Southern Cross and Collingwood supporters with everyone else.*
>
> – *Sydney Morning Herald*, 1 December 2010

spin control

a method of controlling the point of view presented in the media, especially in relation to politics.

Think 'Scotty from Marketing'.

spin doctor

someone who practises **spin control**, especially for another person such as a political candidate.

sportswashing

the practice of a controversial government hosting a popular international sporting event with the intention of garnering the associated favourable attention and thus rehabilitating its poor global reputation.

While there are also the practices of **straightwashing**, **humane washing** and **pink** or **rainbow washing**, it is **sportswashing** and **sanewashing** that feature in the political arena.

> *As the amount of sportswashing increases, authoritarian states may find themselves facing an uphill battle as many sport fans become increasingly socially conscious and more demanding of athletes, leagues, and teams.*
>
> – *The Conversation*, 19 July 2024

stage-manage

to contrive unobtrusively to produce a particular response, as at a political meeting.

stalking horse

a candidate used to screen a more important candidate or to draw votes from and hence cause the defeat of a rival, especially in the US.

strollout

the rollout of the COVID-19 vaccination program in Australia, with reference to the perceived lack of speed.

A humorous blend of *stroll* and *rollout*. For only the second time, the People's Choice was the same as the Committee's Choice, and it was a clear winner, way ahead of the rest of the field. **Strollout** has two levels: at one level it's got a transparency and a play on words, but at that deeper level, when you think about the significance of it, it's a really important marker for this time in Australia's history.

COVID-19, or otherwise known as **the Rona, the spicy cough** and **the boomer remover**.

It's 'not a race' and it's 'not a game show'. But maybe our vaccine strollout is another Borat Subsequent Moviefilm? 'Even Borat is beating Scott Morrison,' Jason Clare complained from his locky d in western Sydney. The Labor frontbencher pointed to Khazakstan's [sic] 66th position on the international vaccine leaderboard, which is well ahead of Australia's 78th.

– *The Australian*, 4 August 2021

sunshine journalism

journalism devoted to presenting positive and heartwarming stories in order to assist a country or its government to overcome problems, assist growth, etc.

Confusingly it is also used to mean journalism which airs topics which others may prefer to keep hidden, as stories based on leaked information.

The second sense relates to the US term **sunshine law** – a state or federal statute requiring that government meetings, decisions, and records be made available to the public.

T

But the root cause of the problem goes back to the 30 years of coalition policy, to the fact that those opposite could not operate a tart shop, much less try to manage a sophisticated industrial economy.

Paul Keating

House of Representatives, Hansard, 11 March 1986

talk out

to thwart the passage of a piece of legislation by prolonging discussion until the adjournment. In the ballpark of **filibustering**.

talking shop

another name for parliament.

tart shop

political office, especially viewed as something to be exploited.

If one is **occupying the tart shop** then they are holding office or occupying a position of power.

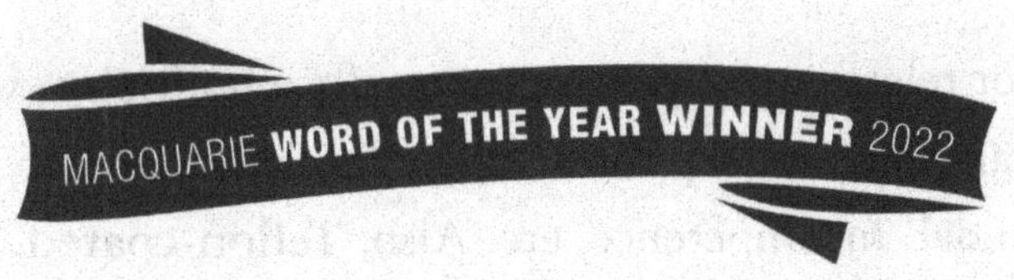

Teal

an independent political candidate who generally supports economic liberalism, but who supports strong action in relation to the environment and climate change, and advocates the prioritising of integrity in politics.

> *Former PM John Howard last week grumped that the teals were nothing more than a mob of "anti-Liberal groupies".*
>
> – *ABC News*, 7 April 2022

It was hard to go past **Teal** as an emblem of Australia's political landscape in 2022. While it wasn't a brand-new word it was a brand-new sense that no-one saw coming. The **Teal** independents won seven seats in the House of Representatives and one seat in the Senate. Called **Teals** from the use of the colour in the candidates' electoral material – thought by some to be representing a mix of blue (Liberal Party) and green (Australian Greens) politics.

Teflon

of or relating to a person, especially a politician, who retains a positive public image despite reports of scandal, incompetence, etc. Also, **Teflon-coated**.

From the synthetic plastic **Teflon**, best known for its non-stick properties on cookware.

the Bush Capital

a humorous name for the city of Canberra, reflecting its natural surroundings and green areas.

Occasionally also referred to as **the Berra, the Can, Cabtown**, and if you want to be rude, **Toy Town**.

there's no such thing as a free lunch

an expression used to communicate the view that anything which appears to be free will in fact have hidden costs attached.

Toy Town

a derogatory term for the city of Canberra, the ACT local government and parliament.

Originally used by people who considered that the territory's small size and lack of industry didn't warrant a parliament.

tree hugger

a derogatory term for an environmentalist.

The term **tree hugger** is the original 'hugger' term. It is also used in a derogatory manner in **coal hugger** and **panda hugger**.

In Senator Bernardi we have six-and-a-half foot of ego but not an inch of integrity.

— Richard Di Natale on Cory Bernardi, Senate, Hansard, 7 February 2017

tree tory

a supporter of the green movement who puts conservative issues ahead of ecological issues.

Confusingly, **tree tory** is also used to refer to a political conservative who cares about the environment, climate action, etc.

The first sense is from the notion that they are *green* on the outside and *blue* on the inside. The second sense is from the notion that they are *blue* on the outside and *green* on the inside.

Compare **watermelon**.

trendy

someone who self-consciously adopts a set of avant-garde social or political viewpoints.

This loose term is most often used pejoratively to describe younger middle-class voters and political activists with little or no sympathy for the traditional values of the major parties. Australian **trendies** tend to be concerned about issues such as the environment, animal liberation, nuclear disarmament, uranium mining, sexual freedom, and other quality of life issues.

trimmer

someone whose support of a political party is determined by expediency rather than firm belief.

truther

a person who believes that what is commonly held to be fact is, in reality, not true at all but the result of a conspiracy by government or some similar authority, designed to keep the real truth from the people, as, for example, the belief that the terrorist attacks on the US on 11 September 2001 were the work of, or condoned by, the US government. See **QAnon**.

tub-thumper

a heavy-handed and ranting public speaker.

turncoat

someone who changes party or principles; a renegade.

The Treasurer is like a souffle which has waited too long for the top job: he has gone flat and even his most odious sycophants will soon appreciate that.

Alexander Downer on Paul Keating
Press Release, January 1988

un-Australian

of conduct, behaviour, beliefs, etc., not conforming to ideas of traditional Australian morality and customs, such as fairness, honesty or hard work.

Violation or perceived breach of any of these unspoken codes is the gravest of sins and may incur this weighty slur.

undorse

to make public one's negative opinion of a politician.

V

Maybe I know nothing about politics, but if this is getting you votes, I am a Martian astronaut!

—

Bob Katter on the China-Australia Free Trade Agreement

House of Representatives Hansard, 21 October 2015

virtue signalling

an expression of opinion, either favourable or unfavourable, which is intended to indicate to others that the person uttering it holds views in line with what is considered to be correct, thus promoting their social standing.

A behaviour both demonstrated and called out by all sides of politics, often seen to be about showcasing one's values rather than driving substantial change.

No country is ever going to hit net zero without some very creative accounting. Whatever Australia does will be a futile and staggeringly expensive exercise in virtue signalling that will not make a jot of difference to the climate.

– *The Australian*, 17 May 2025

vote bait

a policy that is superficially attractive though of little real merit, designed to appeal to voters during an election.

vote stacking

the manipulation of a voting procedure by gathering together a large number of voters who will all vote in a particular way.

There is a danger of putting Parliament House on the lake because there are far too many people in this place who believe they, too, can walk on the water.

Sir James Killen
Sydney Morning Herald, 1 August 1968

walk back

to distance oneself from a previous statement or position.

Also, regularly called a **backtrack** but more tentative than a **backflip**.

water-cooler topic

a topic of general interest and concern.

From the notion that discussion of such a topic

occurs as people in an office gather for a drink of water. Originally a US term which has made its way Down Under. A watered down form of our **barbecue stopper**.

watermelon

a derogatory term for a supporter of the green movement who puts social justice issues ahead of ecological issues.

So called from the notion that they are *green* on the outside and *pink* (leftist-leaning) on the inside. Compare **tree tory**.

WAxit

the movement for the state of Western Australia to secede from the Australian Federation.

Modelled on **Grexit**, **WAxit** is a blend of **W(estern) A(ustralia)** and **exit**. Queensland liked this idea and formed their own **Quexit**.

weasel words

any equivocating or ambiguous words which rob a statement of its force.

Weasel words are one of the techniques employed in **doublespeak** in order to dilute, obscure or just confuse the meaning of what is being communicated.

wedge politics

a political strategy whereby one group seeks to weaken opposing groups by forcing them to divide over a particular issue rather than form an alliance.

wheeling and dealing

intense negotiations in business or politics.

The **wheeler-dealer** being in a position of power to control and direct the actions of others.

Justin Trudeau
AKA
Tru-daddy
Mr Dressup

whistleblower

a person, usually an employee or member of an organisation, who alerts the public to some scandalous practice or evidence of corruption of that organisation.

white

in some European countries, royalist, reactionary, or politically extremely conservative.

Compare **red** and **pink**.

white-ant

to subvert or undermine from within an organisation or enterprise.

white bread

lacking conviction, especially as a consequence of having no varied life experience before becoming a career politician.

Also, a derogatory term to designate an approach to politics which is essentially conservative and monocultural.

The leader of the opposition is the Mr Potato Head of the Australian politics. You can put whatever face you like on the Leader of the Opposition.

– *Christopher Pyne on Bill Shorten, House of Representatives, Hansard, 24 March 2014*

wholesale politics

the employment of mass marketing techniques to further the interests of a political party, cause, etc., as in television and internet advertising, direct mail, telemarketing, etc. Compare **retail politics**.

Despite reportedly spending $60 million campaigning for the 2025 federal election, Clive Palmer's Trumpet of Patriots party failed to win a single seat in the House of Representatives.

woke

a term now used to instantly denigrate and label people or attitudes as overly progressive or liberal.

An interesting example of how quickly language can shift and be weaponised as a means of attack. Originally something to aspire to, meaning 'sensitive to or keenly aware of prejudice and how it is manifested in society', now anyone can be instantly dismissed by slapping a label of **wokeness**, **wokeism** or **wokery** on them.

wokescold

to rebuke a person for having beliefs that are perceived to be accepting of prejudice or discrimination.

woketard

a **woke** person, especially one who is seen as holding politically and socially progressive views that don't align with one's own.

wolf warrior diplomacy

a perceived diplomatic strategy of China in which criticism from another country is met with an immediate response, retaliation, etc.

The term comes from the 2015 Chinese action and war film *Wolf Warrior*, in which China's national interests are aggressively defended by the state's military special forces.

wombat trail

the events and stops made by a political candidate in rural areas, especially by the National Party of Australia in the lead up to an election.

wonk

an expert in a particular field.

Like the **hawk**, **wonk** can be used of particular specialists, as in a **defence wonk** or **policy wonk**.

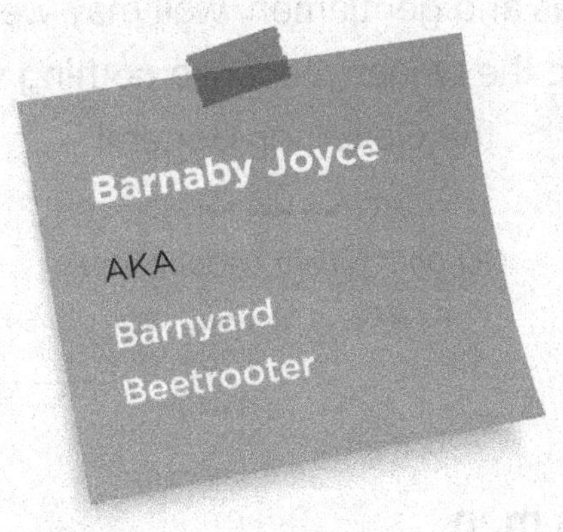

Ladies and gentlemen, well may we say 'God Save the Queen', because nothing will save the Governor-General.

—

Gough Whitlam on John Kerr

ABC News, 11 November 1975

yesterday's man

a man who once was powerful in the affairs of business, politics, etc., but who no longer holds such power.

Zimbabwe option

a government procedure of issuing more money in an attempt to escape a financial crisis.

Quantitative easing gone wild! The term is based on the period of hyperinflation experienced by

Zimbabwe which began in 2007. At its peak, Zimbabwe experienced a month-on-month inflation rate of around 79.6 billion per cent. They also issued a 100 trillion Zimbabwean dollar note which, at the time of its circulation, might only buy a bus fare. It serves as a warning about the dangers of excessive printing of money. Taking the **Zimbabwe option** never ends well.

zombie measure

a measure introduced by a government which has been blocked in the parliament but which is still part of the government's strategy and calculations.

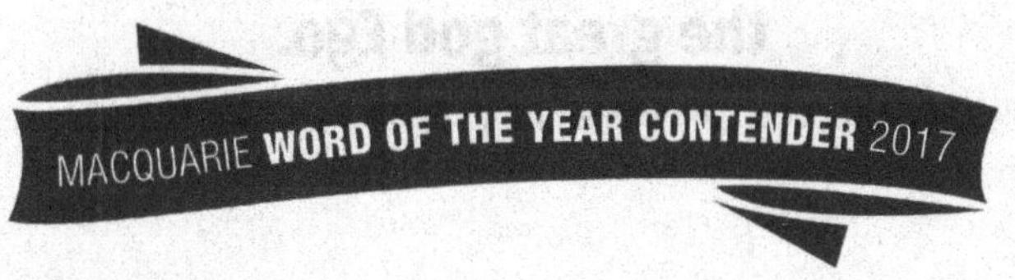

zombie savings

savings in a budget which a government claims it will make but which are dependent on measures which are unlikely to be passed by parliament.

The government will now be forced to remove the $13.2bn in so- called zombie savings from its budget books in May due to concerns that the *ratings agencies will not accept them as genuine savings and lower the nation's AAA credit rating.*

– *The Australian*, 16 February 2017

Taken in the mass our side are a lot of boneheads, and the other side a lot of uncouth, semi-educated, ill-mannered, narrow-minded boors ... At least they work as a team, well-organized, which is more than we can say for ourselves. No handle but that of the parish pump is ever grasped – barring that of the beer pump. It is all what is best for me, myself, the great god Ego.

– *Wilfred Kent Hughes upon entering the Victorian Legislative Assembly, 1927*